mental_floss
SUDOKU

It's the *brain candy* you've been *craving!*

FRANK LONGO

PUZZLE
WRIGHT
PRESS

New York

PUZZLE
WRIGHT
PRESS
New York

An Imprint of Sterling Publishing
387 Park Avenue South
New York, NY 10016

ISBN 978-1-4027-8939-7

Distributed in Canada by Sterling Publishing
c/o Canadian Manda Group, 165 Dufferin Street
Toronto, Ontario, Canada M6K 3H6
Distributed in the United Kingdom by GMC Distribution Services
Castle Place, 166 High Street, Lewes, East Sussex, England BN7 1XU
Distributed in Australia by Capricorn Link (Australia) Pty. Ltd.
P.O. Box 704, Windsor, NSW 2756, Australia

For information about custom editions, special sales, and premium and
corporate purchases, please contact Sterling Special Sales at 800-805-5489 or
specialsales@sterlingpublishing.com.

Printed in China

10   9

www.puzzlewright.com

CONTENTS

INTRODUCTION

To solve sudoku puzzles, all you need to know is this one simple rule:

Fill in the boxes so that the nine rows, the nine columns, and the nine 3×3 sections all contain every digit from 1 to 9.

And that's all there is to it! Using this simple rule, let's see how far we get on this sample puzzle at right. (The letters at the top and left edges of the puzzle are for reference only; you won't see them in the regular puzzles.)

	A	B	C	D	E	F	G	H	I
J									
K					2		1	8	4
L	9		5		7		2		6
M	1		4	3	9	2		7	
N				7		6			
O		7		1	4	8	9		2
P	3		2		6		8		5
Q	8	4	9		3				
R									

The first number that can be filled in is an obvious one: box EN is the only blank box in the center 3×3 section, and all the digits 1 through 9 are represented except for 5. EN must be 5.

The next box is a little trickier to discover. Consider the upper left 3×3 section of the puzzle. Where can a 4 go? It can't go in AK, BK, or CK because row K already has a 4 at IK. It can't go in BJ or BL because column B already has a 4 at BQ. It can't go in CJ because column C already has a 4 at CM. So it must go in AJ.

Another box in that same section that can now be filled is BJ. A 2 can't go in AK, BK, or CK due to the 2 at EK. The 2 at GL rules out a 2 at BL. And the 2 at CP means that a 2 can't go in CJ. So BJ must contain the 2. It is worth noting that this 2 couldn't have been placed without the 4 at AJ in place. Many of the puzzles rely on this type of stepping-stone behavior.

We now have a grid as shown.

Let's examine column A. There are four blank boxes in column A; in which blank box must the 2 be placed? It can't be AK because of the 2 in EK (and the 2 in BJ). It can't be AO because of the 2 in IO. It can't be AR

	A	B	C	D	E	F	G	H	I
J	4	2							
K					2		1	8	4
L	9		5		7		2		6
M	1		4	3	9	2		7	
N				7	5	6			
O		7		1	4	8	9		2
P	3		2		6		8		5
Q	8	4	9		3				
R									

because of the 2 in CP. Thus, it must be AN that has the 2.

By the 9's in AL, EM, and CQ, box BN must be 9. Do you see how?

We can now determine the value for box IM. Looking at row M and then column I, we find all the digits 1 through 9 are represented but 8. IM must be 8.

	A	B	C	D	E	F	G	H	I
J	4	2							
K					2		1	8	4
L	9		5		7		2		6
M	1		4	3	9	2		7	8
N	2	9			7	5	6		
O		7		1	4	8	9		2
P	3		2		6		8		5
Q	8	4	9		3				
R									

This brief example of some of the techniques leaves us with the grid at right.

You should now be able to use what you learned to fill in CN followed by BL, then HL followed by DL and FL.

As you keep going through this puzzle, you'll find it gets easier as you fill in more. And as you keep working through the puzzles in this book, you'll find it gets easier and more fun each time. The final answer is shown below.

This book consists of 246 puzzles in these levels:

—FRANK LONGO

	A	B	C	D	E	F	G	H	I
J	4	2	1	6	8	3	5	9	7
K	7	3	6	5	2	9	1	8	4
L	9	8	5	4	7	1	2	3	6
M	1	5	4	3	9	2	6	7	8
N	2	9	8	7	5	6	4	1	3
O	6	7	3	1	4	8	9	5	2
P	3	1	2	9	6	7	8	4	5
Q	8	4	9	2	3	5	7	6	1
R	5	6	7	8	1	4	3	2	9

Puzzle 1

		5		4				6
9	4			2	6			5
		6					2	
				8	2	1		
4	2						5	8
		1	3	7				
	6					5		
7			5	3			1	2
8				1		9		

Puzzle 2

			2			8		1
8						3	9	
1				5	3	6		
	3	1			6			
	7			2			1	
			4			5	2	
		2	7	3				8
	6	5						9
7		8			2			

7			2			4		3
2	3			1				
	4	8	5					
	5					6		4
8			6		3			9
4		2					3	
					9	8	6	
				7			9	5
5		6			1			7

6		7					8	
	5	3						4
			6		2			7
	3			9	4	6		
	1			7			2	
		4	1	5			3	
8			9		3			
1						8	5	
	4					9		1

5

2	1			7			4	
			3	2	1		5	
8			4					6
3		8				7		
		1				5		
		7				9		4
1					4			3
	3		6	1	2			
	4			8			7	2

6

1	4				3	9		
				8	9		2	
	8	9	6		7			
3		2					1	
6								7
	9					3		2
			2			8	1	3
	5		9	3				
		3	1				4	5

Puzzle 7:

9		8						
1			3				9	5
			9	7		3	8	
		4		3				
	1	2	8		7	4	3	
				1		6		
	5	7		2	8			
3	4				6			2
						1		7

7

Puzzle 8:

8			6				7	
		1	2	4				
7			8			1	3	
3			4				6	
		7		5		3		
	4				3			9
	6	3			8			1
			6	9	2			
	7				4			8

8

			1				8	2
8	5	7						9
		1		9	5			
	1	9		6				
6			2		3			4
				4		6	7	
			4	8		9		
7						3	4	6
9	6				7			

3					1	5		
1						9		6
			5	4	3		1	
	9	3				7		
	1		2		5		9	
		7				1	5	
	3		6	5	8			
6		9						1
		8	4					5

Puzzle 1/1:

9	7			6				
			3		1			7
	4	2	8					
	5	8						9
3		7	4		5	6		8
2						3	5	
					2	4	7	
7			1		3			
				9			6	1

Puzzle 1/2:

4			3	8				
		8		2	7		3	5
		2					1	
	8					6	5	7
			8		3			
5	9	1					8	
	6					7		
7	2		5	6		1		
				1	4			2

Puzzle 1/3

	4			2	7			
			8			6	2	
1	5					9		8
			3				5	1
		9				4		
7	2				4			
9		4					8	3
	6	3			1			
			2	3			4	

Puzzle 1/4

	1	8	9					
4	5	2		8				
		7			4		5	1
5								9
1			5		8			2
8								3
6	8		1			4		
				7		1	3	6
				5	9	2		

Puzzle 1/5:

4		1						5
	3		7					8
			3	2	5			7
6	9		2					
	4	2				7	8	
					3		9	2
5			9	8	2			
8					1		2	
7						8		9

Puzzle 1/6:

8				6	2		4	
7		1				9		
		6	7					5
					7	5	2	
	6			8			7	
	7	3	9					
6					3	1		
		9				4		7
	4		2	9				6

Puzzle 1/7

			5	6		7	1	
		8	2			9	6	5
6			9	1				
	5					6		
8								4
		9					5	
				4	2			7
2	6	3			9	1		
	9	7		8	3			

Puzzle 1/8

			8	7	3			5
	5	3					2	
6	7	1				3		
				5	8			
3			7		2			4
			9	1				
		4				1	8	3
	9					5	7	
2			1	8	5			

1		5				3		
7			1	6				
	6				4	7	1	
3		6		9				
	5		7		8		6	
				4		5		2
	2	7	8				4	
				2	5			7
		3				6		9

		5			2		8	
4					8		5	
9				5		3		
	9				7			4
6		1				5		2
2			1				9	
		8		4				1
	6		7					5
	3		2			4		

Puzzle 2-1

		9	8			1		
					1	2	8	
8	4							6
	5	6		9	3			
2				1				7
			4	7		5	9	
6							1	8
	7	8	1					
		2			5	9		

Puzzle 2-2

	9		2	5				
2						7	1	
3		1		9			2	
					3	5		
8	7		5		4		6	2
		4	7					
	4			2		1		6
	2	3						8
			3	5		4		

Puzzle 2/3:

3				6		1		
			8	5	4		7	
4	9					6	2	
			1			7	4	
			4		6			
	2	4			3			
	4	1					6	8
	3		7	8	9			
		2		4				7

Puzzle 2/4:

		5					3	8
		1		4	3			6
9		3					1	
	3			1	7		6	
	5						8	
	6		4	3			2	
	8					6		7
3			6	7		1		
7	1					8		

2/5

			6	8		3		
					9	5		2
6	1					7		
9	4			5	1			
7	3						5	1
			7	3			4	6
		1					8	5
5		3	8					
		7		1	6			

2/6

			3					8
	3	5	4	1				2
			2			4		
	1					5	7	4
			3	2	4			
9	6	4					8	
		9			3			
4				8	1	7	9	
8				7				

27

3			6	7				
9	5		3					4
		7			8		3	
		1		4			8	
	8	6				3	9	
	3			1		4		
	1		7			8		
7					9		4	6
				6	4			3

28

		7	8	9				
		1					4	6
	4			2	1			
3		4			2			8
2			3		6			5
8			5			2		9
			1	6			8	
4	8					7		
			7	8	9			

Puzzle 29

			6	5		3		2
	1			7			6	
	2	5						7
			8		5	7		
8	3						9	5
		9	3		1			
3						8	5	
	6			1			2	
1		4		8	9			

Puzzle 30

5	9		1					
	4	6		7				
2			4			5	8	3
6				9				
		3	2		7	6		
				8				9
7	1	5			8			2
				5		7	9	
				6			4	5

Puzzle 3-1:

4				9	1			
	5				4	7		
3	7			5	2	9		4
						2	3	
		7				4		
	8	1						
6		4	9	2			7	8
		3	5				2	
			8	1				9

Puzzle 3-2:

9		7				1		
	6					9	2	
			9		6			4
	1			7	3		4	
7		8				3		2
	5		2	1			8	
4			1		8			
	7	3					9	
		1				5		8

		8	6	4				7
4	7						6	
	3							1
		2		6	4	8		
	9		8		7		3	
		7	2	3		9		
7							8	
	5						1	3
8				1	9	2		

			2	3			6	
	2	8				9	7	
	6					3		8
8	7		5					
2			6		9			7
					1		5	3
5		7					4	
	9	2				7	3	
	1			9	6			

Puzzle 3/5

6			4		3			
		4	6				5	3
9		7					6	
	2	5		9				
7				6				8
				8		3	7	
	6					7		4
4	1				2	9		
			8		6			5

Puzzle 3/6

	4		1			3		
				8	7	5		
		7			4			1
			7			4	5	3
4	7						2	9
3	9	5			1			
9			3			6		
		8	5	7				
		4			9		8	

9	5			3				
1			9	5			4	
4		2	1					
		9			4		1	
	4	5				9	7	
	2		3			6		
					8	7		2
	8			6	9			1
			1				5	6

			5	6	8			
1	8		9					
	5	2				9		
3	4	5					1	
7				3				2
	1					4	3	6
		3				1	8	
					6		2	3
			7	4	3			

Puzzle 39

2	5					4		
	3	8	2	6		5		
	4		3					8
4					9			
5				1				2
			5					3
3					2		9	
		5		9	3	2	8	
		4					1	7

Puzzle 40

	7	8			2			
		9	7			5		4
		5				7	8	
8			5	3				
		4		6		9		
				4	7			5
	2	6				8		
5		1			3	2		
			4			3	5	

Puzzle 4-1

					8	7		1
	9			1			3	
		6			7			
1			8			6		
	6	5		4		3	9	
		9			2			4
			2			9		
	3			7			8	
8		7	6					

Puzzle 4-2

6					3		7	2
3							6	
					9	4		
5		3		2		6	1	
			9		1			
	1	7		4		9		3
		5	7					
	8							6
2	4		3					8

Puzzle 4-3:

5	7			6	8	1		
				1		6		
1		4	7				8	2
								5
	1		5		6		2	
9								
7	2				9	5		1
		8		5				
		1	4	7			3	9

Puzzle 4-4:

| 4 | 3 |

| 4 | 4 |

| Puzzle 4-4 grid |

		9			2		7	6
	5	6		9				
2					7			
	2	1						7
	8	3				5	1	
6						8	9	
			9					4
				4		6	8	
4	7		2			3		

Puzzle 4/5:

		3	2				5	
8			6			1	3	
						2	6	4
			1	8				
4	8		2				7	6
			7	3				
9	1	8						
	5	7			9			1
	3				1	5		

Puzzle 4/6:

1	3		9			4	8	
9			3					
		6			1			
3			7				2	8
	4			5			9	
7	6				9			3
			5			2		
					7			9
	5	1			2		7	6

3						4		2
		7	4					
5			2		6	1	3	
1				6			8	
	8			4			2	
	5			2				9
	1	4	3		8			5
					2	3		
2		5						7

		2	8					5
		8	6				1	
5	7	9				6		
			5	9				4
			2		4			
4				3	6			
		4				8	3	1
	1				5	2		
6					2	9		

Puzzle 49:

7			2	8				
			1				6	9
		9	3				1	2
2	6	8				9		
1								7
		3				2	5	1
5	8				7	1		
6	3				1			
			6	2				3

Puzzle 50:

	6						2	
2			7		9	8		3
		4		2				6
			2	5		3		
	3	7				2	5	
		6		8	1			
1				3		5		
7		5	8		2			4
	8						1	

Puzzle 5-1:

	7		8			6		
3	2			4				
1			2	9				7
		3	9					
8	9	6				2	1	4
					1	3		
9				3	4			1
				7			4	2
		1			9		8	

Puzzle 5-2:

				5				4
	9				3	1		
6		1			2	7	8	
1	6	4						
			3	4	5			
						8	4	9
	5	9	8			2		3
		8	6				9	
3				2				

		9	3					4
	4					8		
			4	9	5		6	7
				1		6		3
	7	3				2	1	
9		8	2					
3	5		2	7	6			
		6					5	
2				8		3		

		4	1				6	3
5		6				2		
1					3		5	
				9	6		4	
		7		5		6		
	5		3	8				
	7		5					4
		5				9		2
9	8				2	5		

Puzzle 5-5:

				3		4		5
3			1		5			
		2	6				3	
					8		9	1
6	1	9				3	8	4
8	3		4					
	9				3	2		
			2		4			6
4		5		7				

Puzzle 5-6:

8			6		2	3		
1		5				4		
	3			4		5		
			7	1				3
	2		4		9		1	
4				8	3			
		9		2			5	
		8				9		2
		1	3		6			4

6	5					9		
	8		5	9				
		1			4			6
		4			5			2
9	6						5	4
3			7			6		
7			8			4		
				2	3		8	
		2					6	5

7				8	9		6	
	2	1					4	
9		4	6					7
			8			3		4
	3						9	
1		6			7			
2					3	7		8
	7					4	2	
	1		2	7				3

Puzzle 59

	8		4			1		
4				9			2	8
	9	1		8				
	3				8			1
		7				2		
1			5				7	
				4		9	5	
8	2			6				3
		6			9		1	

Puzzle 60

			9	3		8		
				4	8	1	9	
9	6			5		3		
8						4		
1	5						8	7
		9						3
		6		8			1	4
	8	5	1	2				
		3		7	9			

6 / 1

				8	3			
	5		9					
8		2		6			5	
					8	9		2
9		5				7		6
6		4	7					
	4			3		5		9
					9		7	
1			4	7				

6 / 2

	7				2	4		
5		9		6		3		7
	1				7	5		
	4		1					
7		5				2		1
				4		3		
		1	8			2		
8		7		4		1		3
		4	9				8	

Puzzle 1:

	2	9	5		8			
7	5					8		
3				6				9
4					9		2	
	9	3				6	1	
	7		6					3
1				8				6
		4					3	7
			3		1	4	5	

Puzzle 2:

	3				9		1	6
	9			4				3
		5	2			7		
				7	4	3		
3		8				1		4
		6	3	9				
		1			3	4		
5				1			3	
4	2		8				5	

		7		2			1	
	1		5		8			
8		4			1			6
					5			7
	8		1		4		6	
5			8					
2			7			1		8
			9		3		4	
	3			1		5		

2		1	5					
7		9	2			4		1
			4	1	8			
	7							8
			9		2			
8							4	
			8	5	9			
6		5			3	9		2
					1	7		5

Puzzle 1

	4				8			1
6						5		
		5		2	1		4	
8		4	1					
	5			7			8	
					5	4		6
	6		2	3		7		
		7						5
2			4				3	

Puzzle 2

		5					6	
7				2	8			
9	3				4	5		
				1		4	3	
4	2			7			8	5
	1	7		5				
		9	2				1	3
			9	3				2
	5					9		

69

	9		2					5
			5			4	7	2
		5	7	1				
	6	9						
7	8			3			6	1
						9	4	
			6	7	2			
3	7	2			9			
5					8		1	

70

	3	7	5			1		
	5		6	1				
			9					4
6					8		4	
9		8		2		7		5
	2		1					8
7			5					
			8	1			2	
		3			4	8	5	

Puzzle 7-1

1								
2				9		7		
	7		4	1	6	5		
9		1	5			6	7	
	8						2	
	3	5			2	1		9
		2	1	8	3		9	
		4		2				1
								3

Puzzle 7-2

9		2	7				8	
							6	
			2			1		7
		3	6	9				2
	5			4			3	
4				3	1	7		
6		4			5			
	7							
	9				3	5		6

				8		6		2
		7			9	4	8	
							7	5
		1	2	5		9		
	7						3	
		9		7	3	5		
2	1							
	8	5	7			1		
7		4		6				

			6		2	5		4
					5			
	4					3		7
	3					9	6	
		6	1		7	8		
	2	8					3	
4		2					1	
			5					
3		7	4		9			

Puzzle 7-5

	1			8	7			3
	6				2			9
			5			6	7	
					9		3	
5		1				4		6
	7		4					
	5	8			4			
7			8				9	
4			3	6			1	

Puzzle 7-6

	7				6		1	4
	3	6						
4	8					6		
1				2	5			
	6		4		3		9	
			6	9				7
		2					5	9
						1	8	
6	1		9				7	

		9		5			4	8
2	5			9		6		
4				1	7			
						1		
5	4						7	6
		3						
			3	7				2
		4		2			8	9
8	7			6		5		

9							2	3
1		6						
		4		5	2			9
6					4		1	
			6		9			
	1		8					5
7			1	4		2		
						3		1
3	9							7

Puzzle 79

2		5		1		3		8
	1				2			7
6				3			9	
			2					
	8		9	5	3		2	
					8			
	7			2				5
9			3				1	
1		3		4		9		2

Puzzle 80

4			5	7				9
1		9					4	
	5							
		2			1		8	7
			4		3			
5	4		8			2		
							7	
	8					3		4
9				6	4			5

8/1

	2	1			9	7	4	
					4		5	9
					5			
	5						6	8
1		2				9		7
9	4						2	
			6					
8	6		5					
	3	5	2			1	7	

8/2

	6	8					9	2
7					9		6	
				6				7
				9	8	4	7	
		1				3		
	7	2	5	1				
3				2				
	8		6					4
2	4					9	5	

Sudoku 8/3:

7						4		
						2		5
9			3	4	6			8
			7	2			6	
		6				9		
	3			9	5			
6			2	5	9			4
2		8						
		4						1

8/3

Sudoku 8/4:

	5						2	
2						9	8	
8		6	7				3	
			2	3				1
		7	9		6	2		
6				5	4			
	7				5	8		6
	6	5						2
	4						5	

8/4

	4		6	9		2		8
	7		1		4			
				2		4		
								2
9		3				8		7
8								
		6		8				
			5		7		4	
1		7		4	9		8	

1			8		7			9
8			2					
9	3				1		2	4
3		6						
	5		9		8		7	
						4		3
4	2		7				6	5
					2			8
5			6		4			7

Puzzle 87

	9	8		1				3
			7	8				
5	3		6				4	
		2	8					6
3				7				2
8					2	7		
	4				1		9	8
				3	7			
2				4		5	6	

Puzzle 88

7	9							
	4				3	8		
6		5	8	4				
		7		9		1		
8			7	5	2			3
		9		8		5		
				7	1	6		5
		1	6				2	
							1	9

			5					2
6					1	5		
	1			2	8	6		4
			7			3		
	9						4	
		3			2			
4		2	8	7			1	
		1	9					3
7					3			

5			6	4		7	9	
9		8	3			4	1	
			2			6		
8		3					7	
	7					5		3
		9			5			
	8	6			3	9		4
	5	4		7	6			1

Puzzle 91:

	1	7			3	9		
	2							4
3			8				1	
		3				5		1
	9			7			4	
4		1				6		
	4				6			9
2							6	
		9	2			7	8	

Puzzle 92:

8	1	6	2			5		
	2				6			
	4			8				2
6						2	8	
		8		9		6		
	9	3						4
5				2			1	
			6				3	
		1			5	4	2	6

	6				7			9
	8				3	1		
9			8					6
	3			6			8	
		7				2		
	1			5			4	
3					4			2
		5	3				7	
4			1				6	

9			6	2		5		
4	5				7			9
					9	6	3	
3		4					9	
		8				1		
	2					4		3
	4	9	8					
7			3				1	2
		3		1	5			6

Puzzle 9/5:

	2		5	1				6
1	9		6					
	6	8				7		
		4		6				
9				8				2
				4		9		
		2				4	8	
					9		6	7
6				3	4		5	

Puzzle 9/6:

6		7		2			9	
						2		1
9	4		7				6	
				7	6	1		
3								2
	7	1	8					
	6				9		2	5
7		4						
	9			6		8		7

3		5			1		7	
		7	3	5				
		9		8				
4				3		8	2	
		3	1		8	4		
	7	6		4				5
				7		5		
				1	3	2		
	1		8			7		9

			5					
1	3		9					
7						2	1	5
	8		7			9		6
			3		5			
4		1			2		8	
6	1	4						7
					6		5	9
				4				

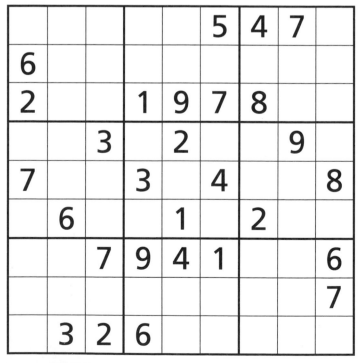

101

	1			4				
6	8					4		3
3		7		1				5
			1	2				6
	7		4		5		3	
5				7	9			
2				9		6		4
1		4					2	9
				3			8	

102

				8			7	
	8							3
3		7	4		1		5	
2	4							
		3	8		6	2		
							6	9
	1		6		8	4		7
5							8	
	7		2					

Puzzle 103

7		8						6
6			2		9		8	3
	9			1		5		7
					6			5
			4		1			
4			5					
5		7		6			9	
9	6		1		4			8
8						1		2

Puzzle 104

3	4	5

			3		4	5		
		9	2	5	1			
	1			9				
5	9						1	2
	3	8				4	7	
2	7						3	8
				3			2	
			4	8	9	3		
		3	5		7			

1					9		4	
		4				2	5	
		6			2		3	1
7	1			4		8		
		9		6			7	2
6	8		1			5		
	9	5				3		
	3		2					7

	4			9				
					7	5	6	
3	7				1		2	
		7						6
9		2				7		4
6						2		
	2		4				3	5
	5	1	3					
				8			1	

	6			4			7	
3				9	6			2
			7			8	1	
6			1					
1				8				7
					3			5
	5	8			9			
2			4	6				1
	1			7			5	

4	6		7		8			
	5			4				
1		7		2		4		
	9						1	4
	1	4				8	9	
5	3						6	
		6		8		3		1
				6			8	
			1		7		2	9

			5			3	1	
			6					2
	9	3			1	6	4	
		6		8		7		
4				6				3
		5		3		4		
	5	4	3			2	9	
1					7			
	6	9			4			

4			9					
		6			7	8		
	1				2			5
	8	7					3	
6	5			7			8	9
	3					7	5	
8			5				2	
		1	4			5		
					1			4

Puzzle 1

		3	2		7		6	9
	8				5	3		4
				8				
		9				4	3	7
8	3	2				6		
				5				
2		6	8				4	
3	7		4		6	5		

1
1
1

Puzzle 2

	1		3		9			
	9			1				
3	2	6	7					
2		4			8	6	9	
	6	8	4			3		7
					2	1	6	3
				3			7	
			8		7		4	

1
1
2

Puzzle 113

5			2		6			7
2		6						
	3				1			
3			1				6	9
				7				
7	5				8			4
			4				1	
						8		5
6			3		5			2

Puzzle 114

6			3			9		
	3	7			2		1	
	2		1	4				5
	4	2						
			4	6	5			
						4	7	
3				7	9		2	
	1		2			3	6	
		4			1			7

Puzzle 115

7				6				
					4	1		
		6	5				3	
1	3				5			8
	7		1		9		6	
5			8				1	7
	4				3	9		
		1	2					
				5				1

Puzzle 116

					6		1	
	2	5				8		
1			3			7		
		2		8	9	6		
5								7
		9	1	5		3		
		6			3			8
		8				2	9	
	9		5					

Puzzle 117:

9		5		3			1	
					5	6		
	6					2	3	
	5						2	
2			5		7			6
	3						7	
	1	8					5	
		9	6					
	7			5		8		9

Puzzle 118:

				2			3	5
			3		6	8		
6				7			4	
			5				6	
5	6						8	4
	3				7			
	5			3				2
		1	4		8			
3	9			5				

7				6		3		
	4	1						6
	2			8		7	9	
		6			4			
	7		6	3	9		4	
			1			9		
	6	5		1			8	
8						4	1	
		2		4				9

			9					
8	5				4	9	7	
	9			5		6		
		3	5	1				4
				6				
4				8	9	7		
		8		9			5	
	1	4	2				9	6
					8			

		6		4		5		
						1	8	
8	7		2			4		
7			9	8				
4								5
			3	7				6
		5			6		4	2
	2	7						
		3		2		7		

		3			8	6		
							9	
		1	2	6			7	
	4		7				6	5
		6				8		
5	3				9		2	
	2			1	4	3		
	7							
		5	8			2		

Puzzle 1:

			7	1				4
			4		5			
	6			8	3			1
	8					5	1	9
6								3
1	9	5					2	
4			8	9			6	
			5		7			
9				6	4			

Puzzle 2:

6		9		3			8	
	2		8				6	
4					6			
		7			4	5		
	1	4		5		9	2	
		6	3			1		
			4					5
	4				7		1	
	3			8		2		4

Puzzle 125

					9			1
	5		2					
	1	9		7				
2				9	8	3		
9		8				1		2
		7	3	5				8
				3		8	4	
					1		6	
8			9					

Puzzle 126

			4					
	6	7	2	5			3	
	3	8			9			
8	7							2
	2	5				7	9	
6							4	5
			1			3	8	
	8			9	7	4	2	
				4				

Puzzle 127:

				2				7
7	9					1		
1		2					5	
	6			9	8			4
8				3				1
3			2	7			6	
	1					2		9
		7					4	8
9				6				

Puzzle 128:

1				9	4		8	
		3			6	5	9	
5								
	6		4				2	8
				6				
4	2				5		3	
								3
	5	7	3			8		
	9		8	4				6

9				3		4	5	
	1	3				2		
		2			8			3
	9				6	5		
		1	7		9	8		
		7	4				9	
4			2			1		
		5				3	4	
	3	9	4					5

				4			8	5
	4	3				1		7
			7	1		2	3	
				5				1
5			2					9
3			7					
	2	5	6	9				
6		8				5	9	
4	3			8				

Puzzle 1

		2	6		7	8		
					1			9
5		7						
2				1				4
1	4		8		9		2	7
6				3				8
						7		5
7			3					
		8	1		4	6		

131

Puzzle 2

6			5			8		2
		5		6		7		
2								
			4	5			6	
	8	2		7		3	4	
	1			9	2			
								8
		7		3		4		
9		8			7			3

132

Puzzle 133:

								8
7	9		5			2		
	3	5	6					4
		4	2		8			
	8			7			2	
			1		3	7		
6						9	3	4
		9			5		1	7
1								

Puzzle 134:

8				5		7		
2	6			9		3		
		1					2	
	3			8	4			
5		8				4		1
			5	2		9		
	5					1		
		3		1			5	4
		6		4				3

Puzzle 1
	5		8	6				
			4		2		7	3
3								5
		9	6		4		5	
	2		5		1	8		
2								9
1	4		2		9			
			3	6		2		

1
3
5

Puzzle 2
4		2			7	1		
			6	8				
				4		9	6	
9		3				8		
5								4
		7				2		3
	9	1		2				
				7	8			
		4	9			3		7

1
3
6

Puzzle 139:

		2	3		6		4	
		7	8				6	
9				2				
8		1			3			4
	7						8	
4			6			1		9
				6				2
	5				2	4		
	4		9		8	7		

Puzzle 140:

				1		9		4
5	4			7	2		6	
		6						8
2	3							
		7		4		2		
							3	7
3						7		
	6		3	5			8	2
1		2		6				

			4		1	5	9	
				8				
	6		7		9		8	
		8				6	3	
	3	4				9	1	
	1	7				8		
	8		3		6		4	
				4				
	5	9	1		7			

		9					4	8
1				4	8			7
						1		
	3	8	7	9		6		5
				8				
7		1		6	4	8	2	
		7						
3			6	5				2
2	5					3		

Puzzle 1 4 3

9	7		6					
1		8						6
	3			7	4			
8	1		9				2	
			3		5			
	6				2		8	7
			4	2			9	
4						7		2
					9		6	5

Puzzle 1 4 4

4	9		5			1		
		5	1					
1				3	6		9	
5		2	9				1	
				2				
	8				1	4		5
	3		2	5				1
					7	2		
		8			4		5	7

145

1	9						3	
5		7		3		1		
					6		9	
	3		2					7
		1				3		
7					4		8	
	5		7					
		3		5		4		9
	7						2	1

146

|
|---|---|---|---|---|---|---|---|---|
| | | | 2 | | | 9 | | |
| | 1 | 8 | | | | | | 4 |
| 5 | | | | | | | 3 | 1 |
| | 7 | | 3 | | 2 | | 5 | 8 |
| | 8 | | | 5 | | | 4 | |
| 4 | 3 | | 8 | | 1 | | 7 | |
| 7 | 9 | | | | | | | 2 |
| 6 | | | | | | 3 | 9 | |
| | | 3 | | | 9 | | | |

Puzzle 147

		7		4		8	2	
	1				2			7
			6			9	3	
		8	2		4			
				5				
			8		1	4		
	8	4			6			
3			5				7	
	5	9		7		1		

1 4 7

Puzzle 148

	3		5			2		
						9	7	
			3				1	
		7	1		5		4	6
8				4				7
6	4		2		7	5		
	9				1			
	7	1						
		2			9		3	

1 4 8

	9		2				1	4
	1		6					
	3		9		1			6
		1				2		3
	2						6	
6		8				4		
7			3		9		2	
					6		7	
3	5				8		4	

			9				3	
	8	6	3		1		4	9
		3	4				7	
8								
4				8				7
								2
	2					3	9	
7	9		8			6	4	1
	6					9		

Puzzle 151

2		6			5			4
8					4			
			2			8		
			6			2	7	
4			3		8			6
	6	5			9			
		4			3			
			4					1
7			1			6		3

1 5 1

Puzzle 152

					7		3	
8			5			7	2	
		1						5
9		7	1					
		6	7		5	8		
					2	1		7
6						4		
	3	2			1			6
	8		3					

1 5 2

Puzzle 153

	2		5		8	7		6
			6				5	
			4		3		9	8
		8				5	3	
			3		2			
	3	4				8		
3	4		2		9			
	5				4			
6		9	8		5		4	

Puzzle 154

		4	8					1
5					7	8	2	
	9		3					
1							3	4
	8	3		4		7	5	
4	5							8
					9		8	
	4	1	6					5
3				5		6		

	7					4		
			3		9		1	
5	2			7			3	
	9		2	4		3		
			7		6			
		2		5	3		9	
	4			3			6	2
	3		5		4			
		5					4	

155

5	6		3				9	
			6	2	9			
4					5			
			2					9
2		7		9		5		3
9					1			
			7					2
			1	3	2			
	8				6		1	7

156

157

		8	4				7	
	4			7	1		8	3
	1					6		
5	7		9					
		6		3		5		
					6		1	9
		7					3	
4	3		1	6			5	
	8				5	4		

158

					9			
			7	3				5
3	1	6			8		2	
2		5			7		8	
	3		8			7		9
	9		3			2	1	4
4				8	6			
			1					

Puzzle 159

9			5					8
	8		3		7		1	4
				8				5
			9			2		
	6	9				7	5	
		3			5			
7				3				
3	5		4		8		9	
6					1			2

Puzzle 160

5			7			1		9
					1	6		
	7				8			5
9			3			2		
	3	4		1		8	9	
		7			9			3
7			1				5	
		3	6					
1		5			4			8

			3			8		5
							1	2
1					8	4	9	
			4	7			5	
4	2						3	6
	8			6	3			
	3	1	5					9
5	7							
8		6			1			

					2	1		7
2	5				7		4	
			5	1				
	2	9		6			7	
			7		8			
	7			3		5	2	
				5	3			
	3		2				8	6
6			7	8				

Puzzle 163

		2		5		1	3	
4				3	9		2	
	3							5
		3	8					
2			3	6	7			8
				5	7			
8							9	
	2		9	4				1
	6	9		1		4		

Puzzle 164

	9				5		4	
5							7	
	4			6		2		
	5	8	6					
		3	5		4	9		
					9	6	3	
		4		7			2	
	3							4
	8		1				9	

165

		6			4			9
4	2			3				
5	9		8					
	6				2			7
		1		5		9		
8			7				4	
					3		6	1
				7			3	2
6			1			7		

166

1							4	
		5				9	7	
			3		7			
	2		8	4				5
	1	8		9		4	3	
3				1	5		8	
			6		2			
	9	2				6		
	6							7

Puzzle 167

9		7	8			5		
								3
			5	6	9			2
		8		5			9	
			6	1	4			
	3			2		6		
1			3	8	6			
7								
		5			7	2		6

Puzzle 168

			3			6		2
			5	1				7
3			2			5		
8		3				2		
			9	8	2			
		4				9		5
		9		8				4
6			5	2				
4		8	1					

	4			8				7
			2	4				8
6					1			2
	1			2	4			
		7				6		
			1	9			8	
7			3					9
3				1	5			
8				7			4	

		6		4	5			
5	7							
9						2		
	8		5		3		6	4
		7	1		4	5		
4	5		6		9		3	
		2						9
							2	8
			3	5		7		

	2			7	1			
	1	9						
7						5		
9			1	5		4		2
		1	9		8	3		
4		5		2	3			1
		6						5
						6	9	
			8	9			3	

	5	2						4
				1				9
	9				6	3	8	
		5			2	9		3
	4			5			7	
2		7	4			6		
	8	3	9				2	
5				2				
9						8	3	

7			1	2			9	
			7					8
		5					2	
2	7		3					
3				9				6
					7		4	3
	6					3		
4					2			
	3			8	5			7

				2		7		
	8				3			
	3	1	8		4			2
						9	2	
8				9				7
	5	6						
1			3		9	6	5	
			4				1	
		5		1				

175

	8		3				9	
		3	1	7				
	5	1						8
2				4			1	
		8				7		
	7			8				9
7						9	5	
				9	1	6		
	4				5		3	

176

	8		3		1			
		3						
2	9			6		1		
		9	8				6	
	4	8	6		2	3	9	
	1				3	4		
		5		4			8	3
						6		
			7		6		1	

		7		2		5		
8					4		9	
	1					6		
			5					2
	7	1	9		2	3	5	
2				7				
		2					8	
	5		1					6
		6		4		9		

				2		9		
		1	7			3		6
	2				3	7	8	
7			8					
	8			4			9	
				5				7
	7	2	1				6	
1		5			9	2		
		8		3				

Puzzle 179

1		5	6			9		3
		3	7		5			
8								
7				3	6			
	5			2			3	
			1	9				4
								9
			4		1	3		
2		8			3	1		6

Puzzle 180

		6			2			5
8					1	6		9
	9				7			
			5				8	
		9				7		
	1				3			
			8				2	
3		2	1					6
5			6			4		

	6					4		
					5		6	
3		5					2	
6			9	7			5	
7								4
	5			6	1			8
	8					9		2
	1		5					
			7				4	

	5	4					8	9
1								
2	7	8	1			6		
		9	2	8				
		2				5		
				5	3	9		
		6			1	3	9	7
								1
7	4					8	6	

1	7			6				
2			3				9	
		9	8					3
				3	6			
	9	5				7	6	
			4	7				
5					2	4		
	4				3			2
			4				1	7

2	8			5				
						6		2
4					9		1	
		2		6	7			
5			9		4			6
			5	2		3		
	3		7					8
1		8						
				4			7	3

Puzzle 185

1								4
		4	6					
5				3		1	6	
		8	2	6				1
			3		9			
2			1	5		3		
	7	1		8				9
					2	8		
8								7

Puzzle 186

				7			1	4
		8	6				5	
	1					2		
	8	9		4				2
			1		9			
5				8		1	3	
		3					2	
	5				1	3		
8	9			6				

Puzzle 187

2			1				4	
			4			1		
		9	7					6
						2	6	
1			9		8			7
	7	6						
3					4	5		
		2			9			
	6				3			8

Puzzle 188

	1			3	9		5	
				5	7			2
6		7						
	6	3	4			5		
8								3
		5			3	6	2	
						3		1
4			2	1				
	7		3	9			4	

		3	4		5			
	7		1				8	
	4	2			3			6
	2							
	9	8		7		3	6	
							9	
4			8			6	7	
	1				2		3	
			3		7	8		

3		4		5			2	
		8				1	7	9
8					6	3	9	
			8		5			
	7	1	4					5
1	8	6				9		
	9			2		8		1

Puzzle 191

			6					9
	4						6	7
9	2				4			8
	7			8				
		2		4		1		
				5			4	
8			1				5	3
2	5						7	
1					9			

Puzzle 192

		3	1					4
4	1		8		5	2		
	9	6				8		
9							6	
			4		8			
	8							3
		2				3	4	
		9	2		4		8	6
7					3	5		

Puzzle 193

6					1			
	9	5					3	1
		4	5		3			6
		8	9					
			8	3	4			
					5	8		
3			2		8	5		
4	1					7	8	
			4					3

Puzzle 194

	4		2					
		5			8		9	1
1					5	2		8
				7	4			
		3	8		2	7		
			6	3				
9		4	5					3
2	1		4			9		
				9		2		

Puzzle 195:

	3	2				5		
1	7				4		8	
4		5	8			1		
7				4	3			
				1				
			2	9				5
		4			5	3		7
	9		4				5	8
		7				4	9	

Puzzle 196:

3		6		5				9
					1			4
	8		3	9				
	6	3				4		2
	9			1			6	
7		2				8	9	
			4	3			5	
4			9					
6				8		9		7

		5		7	1			4
				6		7	1	
	1		4	2				6
9	3	8						
						6	3	8
8				3	2		7	
	6	9		8				
7			5	1		8		

	9		7	2				
	3	6				7		
					6		2	
	1		3	7				
	7	5				3	1	
				1	8		4	
	6		9					
		1				4	8	
				4	1		7	

Puzzle 199:

8		7					5	
	4					1		2
				3	8		7	
				1		2		
4				9				8
		1		6				
	1		9	2				
2		8					3	
	7					4		5

Puzzle 200:

		6	2	1			7	
		2	4		7		5	
								3
	7			2	4			
8		3				5		4
			3	6			9	
6								
	1		6		2	4		
	4			5	1	9		

201

5								6
7				5		1	4	
		6					9	5
1		2	3	6				
			1		5			
			8	2	6			4
6	9					8		
	1	8		7				2
2								7

202

9			2		6			
	7	4						
3		6				1		8
	4		1	6				
7			8		2			1
				5	7		2	
8		3				4		6
						5	7	
			6		4			3

203

				2		8		6
5					4	9		
	1		5					4
3				9		7		
	7						3	
		1		6				2
1					2		9	
		7	6					5
8		3		5				

204

3	2			5	1			
4					3			9
	6				2			
		2					7	
		3				1		
	9					4		
			7				3	
8			5					6
			1	6			8	7

205

206

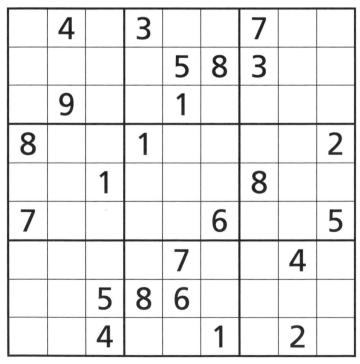

		6	9					
	8				4			3
				7	2			5
1		5				2		
9				2				8
		4				7		6
5			8	9				
3			1				7	
					7	5		

5			3				6	
		7	8	2		5		
		1					8	
3				4				
7			2		9			5
			5					7
	2					1		
		4		8	2	9		
	7				4			2

Puzzle 1

4		9						
				5		3	2	9
			1			8		
	3				2			
		5	9	8	3	1		
			6				7	
		6			1			
9	5	2		3				
						9		7

2 1 1

Puzzle 2

			6				7	
7		3		5		1		
	9	1	4					
	8				5		6	1
2	1		7				4	
					3	8	1	
		4		8		2		5
	5			2				

2 1 2

					8		5	
2				5		7		
3					4	6		
			5			2	1	
5								8
	8	4			2			
		1	3					9
		6		1				7
	9		7					

		4	9		1			
		6						4
					8		2	
5								6
		7	4		6	9		
3								2
	7		6					
8						1		
			5		2	3		

Puzzle 215

	7							8
		5						1
			4	3	1			7
				1		5	9	
			5		6			
	5	2		7				
1			9	4	8			
5						4		
3							2	

Puzzle 216

		4	3			5		
6				9	4			
				1	9	7		
	6							3
				4				
7							2	
	3	1	6					
			4	7				8
		9			5	6		

		1			8	3		
6	9							
				4		6		
			9	6		5		3
		4				2		
2		5		7	1			
	2		1					
							5	7
		8	3			4		

2		7		1				
9						6		7
			2		6			
			4				8	
	3			2			1	
	5				7			
			9		1			
8		4						3
				3		1		6

Puzzle 219

		2	9	7			8	
		8						
		1	5					4
9		3	7					
4				2				6
					3	5		8
8					4	7		
						8		
	2			6	7	1		

Puzzle 220

3		7						
	9		3		4		1	
	8				2		3	
		6				3		
			9		5			
		4				2		
	1		8				4	
	5		6		7		9	
						7		3

221

			4				3	
5			1			7		
	8	7						
					3	1	2	8
1	7	8	5					
						4	6	
		1			6			5
	3				2			

222

	6							8
3		7	4					
			3	2		4		
			9				2	5
	9						3	
7	1				5			
	2		1	7				
				2		4		6
4							1	

Puzzle 223

9		4			7			2
	7			1	6			
		6						
4		5	1			9		
		8			3	2		6
						7		
			9	8			1	
5			2			8		9

Puzzle 224

	5		4					8
		3	8					1
			6					
	1			4			7	
7	4			1			6	9
	3			7			1	
			5					
6				7	2			
1				2		9		

2 2 5

					7	1		
		7						
3	6					4		8
			3			5	4	
9	5			8			3	1
	4	3	6					
6		8					2	4
						6		
		9	1					

2 2 6

5	7		6					
			8			4		
		3	7		2		1	
2		7						
6								9
						8		3
	8		3		4	5		
		2		7				
					1		9	6

7		5		9				6
	9					1		
	4				6			
	8	1	4	2				
3				5				8
				7	8	2	1	
			9				7	
		7					5	
2				6		8		4

	1				7	2		6
		5						3
		2						
	2		4					
6			9		8			7
					3		4	
						8		
7						4		
8		4	2				5	

8			1		3		6	
	7			8	6		5	
	1	4						
		5				8	7	
7				5				1
	9	1				5		
						2	1	
	4		9	7			8	
	8		5		2			7

		7			3		4	
	2		5			7		
6				1	7		3	
							6	4
			2		8			
4	3							
	1		7	3				5
		8			5		7	
	7		9			6		

Puzzle 231

1			5			3		8
						4		9
3		6			9			
			4		6		3	1
9				7				6
7	6		1		5			
			6			8		5
8		2						
6		5			2			3

Puzzle 232

	9			7			8	
5					8			
	3		4		5			2
		9			7		5	
7		2				4		8
	4		8			6		
2			7		9		4	
			3					9
	8			1			3	

Puzzle 1:

	2		6			8		3
4		7	8	9	2			
8						1		
	7	9		1		2	8	
		6						5
			7	4	1	5		2
1		5			9		3	

Puzzle 2:

7		2			8			5
4			2				9	
					5		8	4
				7	9			
9								7
			8	5				
8	4		6					
	7				1			2
1			4			3		6

Puzzle 1:

		2		3	7	5		
		5			4			
4			6	5			7	
	8	9						
	5			6			2	
						3	6	
	1			8	3			4
			7			8		
		7	9	4		6		

2
3
5

Puzzle 2:

4			7					6
	1					9		4
		7		6		2		
		1			6			7
			4		1			
5			8			1		
		2		8		7		
6		5					2	
9					3			8

2
3
6

		1	4		2		3	
8			7					1
	5	3			1			
	9	8					7	3
	4						8	
1	3					4	9	
			5			3	1	
2					9			7
	1		8		4	5		

				1			8	
	8						4	6
		1	9			7	5	3
3			5					1
	5			3			6	
4					1			5
9	2	7			5	3		
8	4						7	
	1			4				

Puzzle 239

2			4			1		
6		8					2	
	9			6				
	2	3	8	9				
		1		4		5		
				1	2	7	9	
				3			8	
	6					2		5
		9			1			4

Puzzle 240

1	8							9
7					9	3		
	3			4	6			8
8	7		5					
	2						5	
					3		9	7
5			9	7			4	
		8	1					5
2							8	6

	1					9		
			8	5				2
		6	1	4				8
		4		1			9	5
	2						7	
8	9			7		2		
9				6	3	1		
1				8	4			
		5					4	

		1	9					
	5						7	
4			2		6			1
	4		3		2	5	1	
		9				4		
	6	3	4		1		9	
3			1		8			7
	8						4	
					4	1		

Puzzle 243

	1					7	6	
		9	1		2			
3		4						
1				8	9	5		4
5		7	2	6				3
						3		7
			5		4	8		
	8	2					4	

Puzzle 244

	8		6	7				4
			5					
	6	7		9				2
		6	2					
	3	4				2	8	
					6	3		
3				6		1	2	
					9			
5				8	3		7	

Puzzle 245

	6				2			
1						7	5	
		8			3		4	
7		1	8				9	
	8				6	4		1
	5		9			3		
	4	2						8
			6				7	

Puzzle 246

3		4		8		2	9	
1				9			4	5
9		5		4		1		
8	5		4	1	9		6	2
	4		8	5	2	9	1	
2	9	1	7	6	3	8	5	4
	1					4		
5				7	4			1
4		8				5		9

Puzzle 1

2	1	5	7	4	3	8	9	6
9	4	8	1	2	6	7	3	5
3	7	6	8	5	9	4	2	1
5	3	9	4	8	2	1	6	7
4	2	7	9	6	1	3	5	8
6	8	1	3	7	5	2	4	9
1	6	3	2	9	7	5	8	4
7	9	4	5	3	8	6	1	2
8	5	2	6	1	4	9	7	3

Puzzle 2

6	4	3	2	7	9	8	5	1
8	5	7	6	4	1	3	9	2
1	2	9	8	5	3	6	4	7
2	3	1	5	9	6	7	8	4
5	7	4	3	2	8	9	1	6
9	8	6	4	1	7	5	2	3
4	9	2	7	3	5	1	6	8
3	6	5	1	8	4	2	7	9
7	1	8	9	6	2	4	3	5

Puzzle 3

7	1	9	2	6	8	4	5	3
2	3	5	9	1	4	7	8	6
6	4	8	5	3	7	9	1	2
9	5	3	1	8	2	6	7	4
8	7	1	6	4	3	5	2	9
4	6	2	7	9	5	1	3	8
3	2	7	4	5	9	8	6	1
1	8	4	3	7	6	2	9	5
5	9	6	8	2	1	3	4	7

Puzzle 4

6	9	7	5	4	1	3	8	2
2	5	3	7	8	9	1	6	4
4	8	1	6	3	2	5	9	7
7	3	8	2	9	4	6	1	5
5	1	6	3	7	8	4	2	9
9	2	4	1	5	6	7	3	8
8	7	5	9	1	3	2	4	6
1	6	9	4	2	7	8	5	3
3	4	2	8	6	5	9	7	1

Puzzle 5

2	1	5	8	7	6	3	4	9
9	6	4	3	2	1	8	5	7
8	7	3	4	9	5	2	1	6
3	2	8	5	4	9	7	6	1
4	9	1	2	6	7	5	3	8
6	5	7	1	3	8	9	2	4
1	8	2	7	5	4	6	9	3
7	3	9	6	1	2	4	8	5
5	4	6	9	8	3	1	7	2

Puzzle 6

1	4	7	5	2	3	9	6	8
5	3	6	4	8	9	7	2	1
2	8	9	6	1	7	4	5	3
3	7	2	8	9	5	6	1	4
6	1	8	3	4	2	5	9	7
4	9	5	7	6	1	3	8	2
7	6	4	2	5	8	1	3	9
8	5	1	9	3	4	2	7	6
9	2	3	1	7	6	8	4	5

Puzzle 7

9	3	8	6	5	2	7	1	4
1	7	6	3	8	4	2	9	5
4	2	5	9	7	1	3	8	6
8	6	4	2	3	9	5	7	1
5	1	2	8	6	7	4	3	9
7	9	3	4	1	5	6	2	8
6	5	7	1	2	8	9	4	3
3	4	1	7	9	6	8	5	2
2	8	9	5	4	3	1	6	7

Puzzle 8

8	9	5	6	3	1	4	7	2
6	3	1	2	4	7	9	8	5
7	2	4	8	9	5	1	3	6
3	1	9	4	8	2	5	6	7
2	8	7	9	5	6	3	1	4
5	4	6	1	7	3	8	2	9
4	6	3	5	2	8	7	9	1
1	5	8	7	6	9	2	4	3
9	7	2	3	1	4	6	5	8

9

3	9	6	1	7	4	5	8	2
8	5	7	6	3	2	4	1	9
2	4	1	8	9	5	7	6	3
4	1	9	7	6	8	2	3	5
6	7	8	2	5	3	1	9	4
5	2	3	9	4	1	6	7	8
1	3	5	4	8	6	9	2	7
7	8	2	5	1	9	3	4	6
9	6	4	3	2	7	8	5	1

10

3	8	2	9	6	1	5	4	7
1	4	5	8	2	7	9	3	6
9	7	6	5	4	3	8	1	2
5	9	3	1	8	6	7	2	4
8	1	4	2	7	5	6	9	3
2	6	7	3	9	4	1	5	8
4	3	1	6	5	8	2	7	9
6	5	9	7	3	2	4	8	1
7	2	8	4	1	9	3	6	5

11

9	7	3	5	6	4	1	8	2
6	8	5	3	2	1	9	4	7
1	4	2	8	7	9	5	3	6
4	5	8	2	3	6	7	1	9
3	9	7	4	1	5	6	2	8
2	6	1	9	8	7	3	5	4
8	1	9	6	5	2	4	7	3
7	2	6	1	4	3	8	9	5
5	3	4	7	9	8	2	6	1

12

4	5	6	3	8	1	2	7	9
9	1	8	6	2	7	4	3	5
3	7	2	4	9	5	8	1	6
2	8	3	1	4	9	6	5	7
6	4	7	8	5	3	9	2	1
5	9	1	2	7	6	3	8	4
1	6	5	9	3	2	7	4	8
7	2	4	5	6	8	1	9	3
8	3	9	7	1	4	5	6	2

13

6	4	8	9	2	7	3	1	5
3	9	7	8	1	5	6	2	4
1	5	2	6	4	3	9	7	8
4	8	6	3	9	2	7	5	1
5	3	9	1	7	8	4	6	2
7	2	1	5	6	4	8	3	9
9	1	4	7	5	6	2	8	3
2	6	3	4	8	1	5	9	7
8	7	5	2	3	9	1	4	6

14

3	1	8	9	5	7	2	6	4
4	5	2	6	8	1	3	9	7
9	6	7	2	3	4	8	5	1
5	2	4	3	1	6	7	8	9
1	7	3	5	9	8	6	4	2
8	9	6	7	4	2	5	1	3
6	8	9	1	2	3	4	7	5
2	4	5	8	7	9	1	3	6
7	3	1	4	6	5	9	2	8

15

4	7	1	6	9	8	2	3	5
2	3	5	7	1	4	9	6	8
9	8	6	3	2	5	1	4	7
6	9	8	2	4	7	3	5	1
3	4	2	1	5	9	7	8	6
1	5	7	8	6	3	4	9	2
5	1	3	9	8	2	6	7	4
8	6	9	4	7	1	5	2	3
7	2	4	5	3	6	8	1	9

16

8	9	5	3	6	2	7	4	1
7	2	1	5	4	8	9	6	3
4	3	6	7	1	9	2	8	5
1	8	4	6	3	7	5	2	9
9	6	2	1	8	5	3	7	4
5	7	3	9	2	4	6	1	8
6	5	8	4	7	3	1	9	2
2	1	9	8	5	6	4	3	7
3	4	7	2	9	1	8	5	6

17

9	4	2	5	6	8	7	1	3
1	7	8	2	3	4	9	6	5
6	3	5	9	1	7	4	8	2
7	5	4	8	2	1	6	3	9
8	1	6	3	9	5	2	7	4
3	2	9	4	7	6	8	5	1
5	8	1	6	4	2	3	9	7
2	6	3	7	5	9	1	4	8
4	9	7	1	8	3	5	2	6

18

9	4	2	8	7	3	6	1	5
8	5	3	6	4	1	9	2	7
6	7	1	5	2	9	3	4	8
4	2	6	3	5	8	7	9	1
3	1	9	7	6	2	8	5	4
7	8	5	9	1	4	2	3	6
5	6	4	2	9	7	1	8	3
1	9	8	4	3	6	5	7	2
2	3	7	1	8	5	4	6	9

19

1	4	5	2	8	7	3	9	6
7	3	8	1	6	9	2	5	4
2	6	9	3	5	4	7	1	8
3	7	6	5	9	2	4	8	1
4	5	2	7	1	8	9	6	3
8	9	1	6	4	3	5	7	2
9	2	7	8	3	6	1	4	5
6	1	4	9	2	5	8	3	7
5	8	3	4	7	1	6	2	9

20

3	7	5	4	9	2	1	8	6
4	1	6	3	7	8	2	5	9
9	8	2	6	5	1	3	4	7
8	9	3	5	2	7	6	1	4
6	4	1	8	3	9	5	7	2
2	5	7	1	6	4	8	9	3
5	2	8	9	4	6	7	3	1
1	6	4	7	8	3	9	2	5
7	3	9	2	1	5	4	6	8

21

3	2	9	8	6	7	1	5	4
5	6	7	3	4	1	2	8	9
8	4	1	9	5	2	7	3	6
7	5	6	2	9	3	8	4	1
2	9	4	5	1	8	3	6	7
1	8	3	4	7	6	5	9	2
6	3	5	7	2	9	4	1	8
9	7	8	1	3	4	6	2	5
4	1	2	6	8	5	9	7	3

22

4	9	7	2	5	1	6	8	3
2	5	6	3	4	8	7	1	9
3	8	1	6	9	7	4	2	5
6	1	2	9	8	3	5	7	4
8	7	9	5	1	4	3	6	2
5	3	4	7	6	2	8	9	1
7	4	5	8	2	9	1	3	6
1	2	3	4	7	6	9	5	8
9	6	8	1	3	5	2	4	7

23

3	5	7	9	6	2	1	8	4
2	1	6	8	5	4	3	7	9
4	9	8	3	1	7	6	2	5
5	6	9	1	2	8	7	4	3
8	7	3	4	9	6	2	5	1
1	2	4	5	7	3	8	9	6
7	4	1	2	3	5	9	6	8
6	3	5	7	8	9	4	1	2
9	8	2	6	4	1	5	3	7

24

6	7	5	1	2	9	4	3	8
8	2	1	5	4	3	9	7	6
9	4	3	7	8	6	2	1	5
2	3	9	8	1	7	5	6	4
4	5	7	9	6	2	3	8	1
1	6	8	4	3	5	7	2	9
5	8	2	3	9	1	6	4	7
3	9	4	6	7	8	1	5	2
7	1	6	2	5	4	8	9	3

25

2	7	9	6	8	5	3	1	4
3	8	4	1	7	9	5	6	2
6	1	5	4	2	3	7	9	8
9	4	6	2	5	1	8	3	7
7	3	8	9	6	4	2	5	1
1	5	2	7	3	8	9	4	6
4	2	1	3	9	7	6	8	5
5	6	3	8	4	2	1	7	9
8	9	7	5	1	6	4	2	3

26

2	4	6	7	3	9	1	5	8
7	3	5	4	1	8	9	6	2
1	9	8	2	6	5	4	3	7
3	1	2	8	9	6	5	7	4
5	8	7	3	2	4	6	1	9
9	6	4	1	5	7	2	8	3
6	7	9	5	4	3	8	2	1
4	2	3	6	8	1	7	9	5
8	5	1	9	7	2	3	4	6

27

3	4	2	6	7	5	9	1	8
9	5	8	3	2	1	7	6	4
1	6	7	4	9	8	5	3	2
2	7	1	9	4	3	6	8	5
4	8	6	2	5	7	3	9	1
5	3	9	8	1	6	4	2	7
6	1	4	7	3	2	8	5	9
7	2	3	5	8	9	1	4	6
8	9	5	1	6	4	2	7	3

28

6	3	7	8	9	4	1	5	2
9	2	1	7	3	5	8	4	6
5	4	8	6	2	1	3	9	7
3	5	4	9	1	2	6	7	8
2	7	9	3	8	6	4	1	5
8	1	6	5	4	7	2	3	9
7	9	2	1	6	3	5	8	4
4	8	3	2	5	9	7	6	1
1	6	5	4	7	8	9	2	3

29

9	8	7	6	5	4	3	1	2
4	1	3	9	7	2	5	6	8
6	2	5	1	3	8	9	4	7
2	4	1	8	9	5	7	3	6
8	3	6	4	2	7	1	9	5
5	7	9	3	6	1	2	8	4
3	9	2	7	4	6	8	5	1
7	6	8	5	1	3	4	2	9
1	5	4	2	8	9	6	7	3

30

5	9	8	1	3	2	4	7	6
3	4	6	8	7	5	9	2	1
2	7	1	4	6	9	5	8	3
6	2	4	5	9	3	8	1	7
9	8	3	2	1	7	6	5	4
1	5	7	6	8	4	2	3	9
7	1	5	9	4	8	3	6	2
4	6	2	3	5	1	7	9	8
8	3	9	7	2	6	1	4	5

31

4	6	2	7	9	1	8	5	3
1	5	9	3	8	4	7	6	2
3	7	8	6	5	2	9	1	4
9	4	6	1	7	8	2	3	5
5	3	7	2	6	9	4	8	1
2	8	1	4	3	5	6	9	7
6	1	4	9	2	3	5	7	8
8	9	3	5	4	7	1	2	6
7	2	5	8	1	6	3	4	9

32

9	8	7	3	4	2	1	5	6
5	6	4	7	8	1	9	2	3
1	3	2	9	5	6	8	7	4
2	1	9	8	7	3	6	4	5
7	4	8	5	6	9	3	1	2
3	5	6	2	1	4	7	8	9
4	9	5	1	3	8	2	6	7
8	7	3	6	2	5	4	9	1
6	2	1	4	9	7	5	3	8

33

1	2	8	6	4	3	5	9	7
4	7	5	1	9	2	3	6	8
9	3	6	5	7	8	4	2	1
3	1	2	9	6	4	8	7	5
6	9	4	8	5	7	1	3	2
5	8	7	2	3	1	9	4	6
7	4	1	3	2	5	6	8	9
2	5	9	4	8	6	7	1	3
8	6	3	7	1	9	2	5	4

34

7	5	9	2	3	8	1	6	4
3	2	8	1	6	4	9	7	5
1	6	4	9	5	7	3	2	8
8	7	1	5	2	3	4	9	6
2	3	5	6	4	9	8	1	7
9	4	6	8	7	1	2	5	3
5	8	7	3	1	2	6	4	9
6	9	2	4	8	5	7	3	1
4	1	3	7	9	6	5	8	2

35

6	5	1	4	2	3	8	9	7
2	8	4	6	7	9	1	5	3
9	3	7	5	1	8	4	6	2
8	2	5	3	9	7	6	4	1
7	9	3	1	6	4	5	2	8
1	4	6	2	8	5	3	7	9
5	6	2	9	3	1	7	8	4
4	1	8	7	5	2	9	3	6
3	7	9	8	4	6	2	1	5

36

8	4	9	1	6	5	3	7	2
1	2	3	9	8	7	5	4	6
5	6	7	2	3	4	8	9	1
2	8	1	7	9	6	4	5	3
4	7	6	8	5	3	1	2	9
3	9	5	4	2	1	7	6	8
9	5	2	3	4	8	6	1	7
6	1	8	5	7	2	9	3	4
7	3	4	6	1	9	2	8	5

37

9	5	8	4	3	6	1	2	7
1	7	6	9	5	2	3	4	8
4	3	2	1	8	7	5	6	9
3	6	9	8	7	4	2	1	5
8	4	5	6	2	1	9	7	3
7	2	1	3	9	5	6	8	4
6	1	3	5	4	8	7	9	2
5	8	7	2	6	9	4	3	1
2	9	4	7	1	3	8	5	6

38

9	3	7	5	6	8	2	4	1
1	8	6	9	2	4	3	7	5
4	5	2	3	1	7	9	6	8
3	4	5	6	9	2	8	1	7
7	6	8	4	3	1	5	9	2
2	1	9	8	7	5	4	3	6
6	7	3	2	5	9	1	8	4
5	9	4	1	8	6	7	2	3
8	2	1	7	4	3	6	5	9

39

2	5	7	9	8	1	4	3	6
1	3	8	2	6	4	5	7	9
6	4	9	3	7	5	1	2	8
4	7	2	6	3	9	8	5	1
5	9	3	4	1	8	7	6	2
8	1	6	5	2	7	9	4	3
3	8	1	7	4	2	6	9	5
7	6	5	1	9	3	2	8	4
9	2	4	8	5	6	3	1	7

40

4	7	8	6	5	2	1	9	3
2	3	9	7	1	8	5	6	4
6	1	5	3	9	4	7	8	2
8	6	2	5	3	9	4	1	7
7	5	4	2	6	1	9	3	8
1	9	3	8	4	7	6	2	5
3	2	6	1	7	5	8	4	9
5	4	1	9	8	3	2	7	6
9	8	7	4	2	6	3	5	1

4/1

4	2	3	9	5	8	7	6	1
7	9	8	4	1	6	5	3	2
5	1	6	3	2	7	8	4	9
1	7	4	8	3	9	6	2	5
2	6	5	7	4	1	3	9	8
3	8	9	5	6	2	1	7	4
6	4	1	2	8	3	9	5	7
9	3	2	1	7	5	4	8	6
8	5	7	6	9	4	2	1	3

4/2

6	5	9	4	8	3	1	7	2
3	7	4	1	5	2	8	6	9
1	2	8	6	7	9	4	3	5
5	9	3	8	2	7	6	1	4
4	6	2	9	3	1	5	8	7
8	1	7	5	4	6	9	2	3
9	3	5	7	6	8	2	4	1
7	8	1	2	9	4	3	5	6
2	4	6	3	1	5	7	9	8

4/3

5	7	2	3	6	8	1	9	4
8	3	9	2	1	4	6	5	7
1	6	4	7	9	5	3	8	2
2	8	6	9	3	7	4	1	5
3	1	7	5	4	6	9	2	8
9	4	5	8	2	1	7	6	3
7	2	3	6	8	9	5	4	1
4	9	8	1	5	3	2	7	6
6	5	1	4	7	2	8	3	9

4/4

8	3	9	4	5	2	1	7	6
7	5	6	1	9	3	2	4	8
2	1	4	8	6	7	9	3	5
5	2	1	3	8	9	4	6	7
9	8	3	6	7	4	5	1	2
6	4	7	5	2	1	8	9	3
1	6	5	9	3	8	7	2	4
3	9	2	7	4	5	6	8	1
4	7	8	2	1	6	3	5	9

4/5

1	6	3	2	9	4	8	5	7
8	4	2	6	5	7	1	3	9
7	9	5	1	8	3	2	6	4
3	7	6	4	1	8	9	2	5
4	8	1	9	2	5	3	7	6
5	2	9	7	3	6	4	1	8
9	1	8	5	6	2	7	4	3
2	5	7	3	4	9	6	8	1
6	3	4	8	7	1	5	9	2

4/6

1	3	2	9	7	6	4	8	5
9	8	4	3	2	5	7	6	1
5	7	6	8	4	1	9	3	2
3	1	9	7	6	4	5	2	8
2	4	8	1	5	3	6	9	7
7	6	5	2	8	9	1	4	3
6	9	7	5	3	8	2	1	4
4	2	3	6	1	7	8	5	9
8	5	1	4	9	2	3	7	6

4/7

3	6	1	5	8	9	4	7	2
8	2	7	4	3	1	9	5	6
5	4	9	2	7	6	1	3	8
1	7	2	9	6	3	5	8	4
9	8	6	1	4	5	7	2	3
4	5	3	8	2	7	6	1	9
7	1	4	3	9	8	2	6	5
6	9	8	7	5	2	3	4	1
2	3	5	6	1	4	8	9	7

4/8

1	6	2	8	7	3	4	9	5
3	4	8	6	5	9	7	1	2
5	7	9	4	2	1	6	8	3
7	2	1	5	9	8	3	6	4
8	3	6	2	1	4	5	7	9
4	9	5	7	3	6	1	2	8
2	5	4	9	6	7	8	3	1
9	1	7	3	8	5	2	4	6
6	8	3	1	4	2	9	5	7

49

7	1	6	2	8	9	3	4	5
3	2	5	1	7	4	8	6	9
8	4	9	3	5	6	7	1	2
2	6	8	7	1	5	9	3	4
1	5	4	9	2	3	6	8	7
9	7	3	6	4	8	2	5	1
5	8	2	4	3	7	1	9	6
6	3	7	5	9	1	4	2	8
4	9	1	8	6	2	5	7	3

50

9	6	8	1	4	3	7	2	5
2	5	1	7	6	9	8	4	3
3	7	4	5	2	8	1	9	6
4	1	9	2	5	7	3	6	8
8	3	7	6	9	4	2	5	1
5	2	6	3	8	1	4	7	9
1	4	2	9	3	6	5	8	7
7	9	5	8	1	2	6	3	4
6	8	3	4	7	5	9	1	2

51

5	7	4	8	1	3	6	2	9
3	2	9	7	4	6	1	5	8
1	6	8	2	9	5	4	3	7
4	1	3	9	6	2	8	7	5
8	9	6	3	5	7	2	1	4
2	5	7	4	8	1	3	9	6
9	8	2	5	3	4	7	6	1
6	3	5	1	7	8	9	4	2
7	4	1	6	2	9	5	8	3

52

8	2	7	1	5	6	9	3	4
4	9	5	7	8	3	1	2	6
6	3	1	4	9	2	7	8	5
1	6	4	9	7	8	3	5	2
9	8	2	3	4	5	6	1	7
5	7	3	2	6	1	8	4	9
7	5	9	8	1	4	2	6	3
2	4	8	6	3	7	5	9	1
3	1	6	5	2	9	4	7	8

53

7	6	9	1	3	8	5	2	4
5	4	1	7	6	2	8	3	9
8	3	2	4	9	5	1	6	7
4	2	5	8	1	7	6	9	3
6	7	3	9	5	4	2	1	8
9	1	8	6	2	3	4	7	5
3	5	4	2	7	6	9	8	1
1	8	6	3	4	9	7	5	2
2	9	7	5	8	1	3	4	6

54

7	9	4	1	2	5	8	6	3
5	3	6	9	4	8	2	1	7
1	2	8	6	7	3	4	5	9
8	1	2	7	9	6	3	4	5
3	4	7	2	5	1	6	9	8
6	5	9	3	8	4	7	2	1
2	7	3	5	6	9	1	8	4
4	6	5	8	1	7	9	3	2
9	8	1	4	3	2	5	7	6

55

9	6	1	8	3	7	4	2	5
3	4	8	1	2	5	6	7	9
5	7	2	6	4	9	1	3	8
2	5	4	3	6	8	7	9	1
6	1	9	7	5	2	3	8	4
8	3	7	4	9	1	5	6	2
1	9	6	5	8	3	2	4	7
7	8	3	2	1	4	9	5	6
4	2	5	9	7	6	8	1	3

56

8	9	4	6	5	2	3	7	1
1	6	5	9	3	7	4	2	8
7	3	2	1	4	8	5	6	9
9	8	6	7	1	5	2	4	3
5	2	3	4	6	9	8	1	7
4	1	7	2	8	3	6	9	5
3	7	9	8	2	4	1	5	6
6	4	8	5	7	1	9	3	2
2	5	1	3	9	6	7	8	4

57

6	5	3	2	1	7	9	4	8
4	8	7	5	9	6	2	1	3
2	9	1	3	8	4	5	7	6
1	7	4	9	6	5	8	3	2
9	6	8	1	3	2	7	5	4
3	2	5	7	4	8	6	9	1
7	3	6	8	5	1	4	2	9
5	4	9	6	2	3	1	8	7
8	1	2	4	7	9	3	6	5

58

7	5	3	4	8	9	1	6	2
6	2	1	7	3	5	8	4	9
9	8	4	6	1	2	5	3	7
5	9	2	8	6	1	3	7	4
8	3	7	5	2	4	6	9	1
1	4	6	3	9	7	2	8	5
2	6	5	9	4	3	7	1	8
3	7	9	1	5	8	4	2	6
4	1	8	2	7	6	9	5	3

59

3	8	2	4	5	6	1	9	7
4	7	5	3	9	1	6	2	8
6	9	1	2	8	7	4	3	5
2	3	4	9	7	8	5	6	1
9	5	7	6	1	3	2	8	4
1	6	8	5	2	4	3	7	9
7	1	3	8	4	2	9	5	6
8	2	9	1	6	5	7	4	3
5	4	6	7	3	9	8	1	2

60

5	4	1	9	3	2	8	7	6
3	2	7	6	4	8	1	9	5
9	6	8	7	5	1	3	4	2
8	3	2	5	9	7	4	6	1
1	5	4	2	6	3	9	8	7
6	7	9	8	1	4	5	2	3
7	9	6	3	8	5	2	1	4
4	8	5	1	2	6	7	3	9
2	1	3	4	7	9	6	5	8

61

7	1	6	5	8	3	2	9	4
4	5	3	9	2	7	8	6	1
8	9	2	1	6	4	3	5	7
3	7	1	6	5	8	9	4	2
9	2	5	3	4	1	7	8	6
6	8	4	7	9	2	1	3	5
2	4	7	8	3	6	5	1	9
5	6	8	2	1	9	4	7	3
1	3	9	4	7	5	6	2	8

62

6	7	3	5	1	2	4	9	8
5	2	9	4	6	8	3	1	7
4	1	8	3	9	7	5	6	2
9	4	6	1	2	3	8	7	5
7	3	5	6	8	9	2	4	1
1	8	2	7	5	4	6	3	9
3	6	1	8	7	5	9	2	4
8	9	7	2	4	6	1	5	3
2	5	4	9	3	1	7	8	6

63

6	2	9	5	7	8	3	4	1
7	5	1	9	4	3	8	6	2
3	4	8	1	6	2	5	7	9
4	1	6	8	3	9	7	2	5
8	9	3	7	2	5	6	1	4
5	7	2	6	1	4	9	8	3
1	3	5	4	8	7	2	9	6
9	8	4	2	5	6	1	3	7
2	6	7	3	9	1	4	5	8

64

2	3	4	7	8	9	5	1	6
6	9	7	5	4	1	8	2	3
8	1	5	2	3	6	7	4	9
9	5	2	1	7	4	3	6	8
3	7	8	6	2	5	1	9	4
1	4	6	3	9	8	2	7	5
7	6	1	9	5	3	4	8	2
5	8	9	4	1	2	6	3	7
4	2	3	8	6	7	9	5	1

65

3	5	7	6	2	9	8	1	4
9	1	6	5	4	8	7	2	3
8	2	4	3	7	1	9	5	6
4	9	1	2	6	5	3	8	7
7	8	3	1	9	4	2	6	5
5	6	2	8	3	7	4	9	1
2	4	9	7	5	6	1	3	8
1	7	5	9	8	3	6	4	2
6	3	8	4	1	2	5	7	9

66

2	4	1	5	9	7	8	6	3
7	8	9	2	3	6	4	5	1
5	3	6	4	1	8	2	9	7
9	7	3	1	6	4	5	2	8
1	5	4	9	8	2	3	7	6
8	6	2	3	7	5	1	4	9
3	2	7	8	5	9	6	1	4
6	1	5	7	4	3	9	8	2
4	9	8	6	2	1	7	3	5

67

7	4	2	5	9	8	3	6	1
6	8	1	7	4	3	5	2	9
3	9	5	6	2	1	8	4	7
8	7	4	1	6	2	9	5	3
9	5	6	3	7	4	1	8	2
1	2	3	9	8	5	4	7	6
5	6	8	2	3	9	7	1	4
4	3	7	8	1	6	2	9	5
2	1	9	4	5	7	6	3	8

68

2	4	5	3	9	1	7	6	8
7	6	1	5	2	8	3	4	9
9	3	8	7	6	4	5	2	1
5	9	6	8	1	2	4	3	7
4	2	3	6	7	9	1	8	5
8	1	7	4	5	3	2	9	6
6	7	9	2	4	5	8	1	3
1	8	4	9	3	7	6	5	2
3	5	2	1	8	6	9	7	4

69

6	9	7	2	8	4	1	3	5
8	3	1	5	9	6	4	7	2
4	2	5	7	1	3	8	9	6
1	6	9	8	4	5	3	2	7
7	8	4	9	3	2	5	6	1
2	5	3	6	7	1	9	4	8
9	1	8	4	6	7	2	5	3
3	7	2	1	5	9	6	8	4
5	4	6	3	2	8	7	1	9

70

8	3	7	5	4	2	1	6	9
4	5	9	6	1	7	3	8	2
2	6	1	8	9	3	5	7	4
6	7	5	9	3	8	2	4	1
9	1	8	4	2	6	7	3	5
3	2	4	1	7	5	6	9	8
7	8	2	3	5	9	4	1	6
5	4	6	7	8	1	9	2	3
1	9	3	2	6	4	8	5	7

71

1	4	3	2	5	7	9	8	6
2	5	6	3	9	8	7	1	4
8	7	9	4	1	6	5	3	2
9	2	1	5	3	4	6	7	8
4	8	7	9	6	1	3	2	5
6	3	5	8	7	2	1	4	9
5	6	2	1	8	3	4	9	7
3	9	4	7	2	5	8	6	1
7	1	8	6	4	9	2	5	3

72

9	6	2	7	1	4	3	8	5
1	4	7	3	5	8	2	6	9
5	3	8	2	6	9	1	4	7
8	1	3	6	9	7	4	5	2
7	5	9	8	4	2	6	3	1
4	2	6	5	3	1	7	9	8
6	8	4	1	7	5	9	2	3
3	7	5	9	2	6	8	1	4
2	9	1	4	8	3	5	7	6

Puzzle 7/3

1	4	3	5	8	7	6	9	2
6	5	7	3	2	9	4	8	1
8	9	2	4	1	6	3	7	5
3	6	1	2	5	8	9	4	7
5	7	8	9	4	1	2	3	6
4	2	9	6	7	3	5	1	8
2	1	6	8	9	4	7	5	3
9	8	5	7	3	2	1	6	4
7	3	4	1	6	5	8	2	9

Puzzle 7/4

8	1	3	6	7	2	5	9	4
2	7	9	3	4	5	1	8	6
6	4	5	8	9	1	3	2	7
7	3	4	2	5	8	9	6	1
5	9	6	1	3	7	8	4	2
1	2	8	9	6	4	7	3	5
4	5	2	7	8	3	6	1	9
9	8	1	5	2	6	4	7	3
3	6	7	4	1	9	2	5	8

Puzzle 7/5

9	1	5	6	8	7	2	4	3
3	6	7	1	4	2	8	5	9
8	4	2	5	9	3	6	7	1
6	8	4	2	5	9	1	3	7
5	9	1	7	3	8	4	2	6
2	7	3	4	1	6	9	8	5
1	5	8	9	7	4	3	6	2
7	3	6	8	2	1	5	9	4
4	2	9	3	6	5	7	1	8

Puzzle 7/6

2	7	5	8	3	6	9	1	4
9	3	6	5	1	4	7	2	8
4	8	1	2	7	9	6	3	5
1	9	4	7	2	5	8	6	3
5	6	7	4	8	3	2	9	1
3	2	8	6	9	1	5	4	7
8	4	2	1	6	7	3	5	9
7	5	9	3	4	2	1	8	6
6	1	3	9	5	8	4	7	2

Puzzle 7/7

7	1	9	6	5	2	3	4	8
2	5	8	4	9	3	6	1	7
4	3	6	8	1	7	2	9	5
9	8	7	5	4	6	1	2	3
5	4	1	2	3	9	8	7	6
6	2	3	7	8	1	9	5	4
1	9	5	3	7	8	4	6	2
3	6	4	1	2	5	7	8	9
8	7	2	9	6	4	5	3	1

Puzzle 7/8

9	5	7	4	6	1	8	2	3
1	2	6	3	9	8	5	7	4
8	3	4	7	5	2	1	6	9
6	7	3	5	2	4	9	1	8
5	4	8	6	1	9	7	3	2
2	1	9	8	3	7	6	4	5
7	8	5	1	4	3	2	9	6
4	6	2	9	7	5	3	8	1
3	9	1	2	8	6	4	5	7

Puzzle 7/9

2	9	5	7	1	4	3	6	8
3	1	8	6	9	2	5	4	7
6	4	7	8	3	5	2	9	1
4	3	6	2	7	1	8	5	9
7	8	1	9	5	3	4	2	6
5	2	9	4	6	8	1	7	3
8	7	4	1	2	9	6	3	5
9	5	2	3	8	6	7	1	4
1	6	3	5	4	7	9	8	2

Puzzle 8/0

4	2	3	5	7	8	6	1	9
1	7	9	2	3	6	5	4	8
8	5	6	1	4	9	7	3	2
3	9	2	6	5	1	4	8	7
7	6	8	4	2	3	9	5	1
5	4	1	8	9	7	2	6	3
2	3	4	9	8	5	1	7	6
6	8	5	7	1	2	3	9	4
9	1	7	3	6	4	8	2	5

8-1

5	2	1	8	6	9	7	4	3
3	7	8	1	2	4	6	5	9
6	9	4	3	7	5	8	1	2
7	5	3	9	1	2	4	6	8
1	8	2	4	5	6	9	3	7
9	4	6	7	8	3	5	2	1
2	1	9	6	4	7	3	8	5
8	6	7	5	3	1	2	9	4
4	3	5	2	9	8	1	7	6

8-2

5	6	8	4	3	7	1	9	2
7	2	4	1	5	9	8	6	3
9	1	3	8	6	2	5	4	7
6	3	5	2	9	8	4	7	1
8	9	1	7	4	6	3	2	5
4	7	2	5	1	3	6	8	9
3	5	6	9	2	4	7	1	8
1	8	9	6	7	5	2	3	4
2	4	7	3	8	1	9	5	6

8-3

7	8	3	5	1	2	4	9	6
4	6	1	9	7	8	2	3	5
9	2	5	3	4	6	7	1	8
5	4	9	7	2	1	8	6	3
1	7	6	4	8	3	9	5	2
8	3	2	6	9	5	1	4	7
6	1	7	2	5	9	3	8	4
2	5	8	1	3	4	6	7	9
3	9	4	8	6	7	5	2	1

8-4

7	5	3	1	8	9	6	2	4
2	1	4	5	6	3	9	8	7
8	9	6	7	4	2	1	3	5
4	8	9	2	3	7	5	6	1
5	3	7	9	1	6	2	4	8
6	2	1	8	5	4	3	7	9
3	7	2	4	9	5	8	1	6
1	6	5	3	7	8	4	9	2
9	4	8	6	2	1	7	5	3

8-5

5	4	1	6	9	3	2	7	8
2	7	8	1	5	4	9	3	6
6	3	9	7	2	8	4	5	1
7	1	4	8	3	6	5	9	2
9	2	3	4	1	5	8	6	7
8	6	5	9	7	2	3	1	4
4	9	6	3	8	1	7	2	5
3	8	2	5	6	7	1	4	9
1	5	7	2	4	9	6	8	3

8-6

1	6	2	8	4	7	5	3	9
8	4	5	2	9	3	7	1	6
9	3	7	5	6	1	8	2	4
3	1	6	4	7	5	9	8	2
2	5	4	9	3	8	6	7	1
7	9	8	1	2	6	4	5	3
4	2	1	7	8	9	3	6	5
6	7	9	3	5	2	1	4	8
5	8	3	6	1	4	2	9	7

8-7

6	9	8	4	1	5	2	7	3
4	2	1	7	8	3	6	5	9
5	3	7	6	2	9	8	4	1
1	7	2	8	5	4	9	3	6
3	5	9	1	7	6	4	8	2
8	6	4	3	9	2	7	1	5
7	4	5	2	6	1	3	9	8
9	8	6	5	3	7	1	2	4
2	1	3	9	4	8	5	6	7

8-8

7	9	8	2	1	5	4	3	6
1	4	2	9	6	3	8	5	7
6	3	5	8	4	7	2	9	1
2	5	7	3	9	6	1	4	8
8	1	4	7	5	2	9	6	3
3	6	9	1	8	4	5	7	2
9	2	3	4	7	1	6	8	5
5	8	1	6	3	9	7	2	4
4	7	6	5	2	8	3	1	9

89

3	8	4	5	6	7	1	9	2
6	2	7	4	9	1	5	3	8
9	1	5	3	2	8	6	7	4
2	4	6	7	8	9	3	5	1
1	9	8	6	3	5	2	4	7
5	7	3	1	4	2	8	6	9
4	3	2	8	7	6	9	1	5
8	6	1	9	5	4	7	2	3
7	5	9	2	1	3	4	8	6

90

5	3	2	6	4	1	7	9	8
9	6	8	3	5	7	4	1	2
4	1	7	2	9	8	6	3	5
8	9	3	5	1	4	2	7	6
6	4	5	7	3	2	1	8	9
2	7	1	8	6	9	5	4	3
1	2	9	4	8	5	3	6	7
7	8	6	1	2	3	9	5	4
3	5	4	9	7	6	8	2	1

91

8	1	7	4	2	3	9	5	6
9	2	6	7	1	5	8	3	4
3	5	4	8	6	9	2	1	7
6	8	3	9	4	2	5	7	1
5	9	2	6	7	1	3	4	8
4	7	1	5	3	8	6	9	2
7	4	5	3	8	6	1	2	9
2	3	8	1	9	7	4	6	5
1	6	9	2	5	4	7	8	3

92

8	1	6	2	4	3	5	9	7
3	2	9	7	5	6	8	4	1
7	4	5	9	8	1	3	6	2
6	5	4	1	3	7	2	8	9
1	7	8	4	9	2	6	5	3
2	9	3	5	6	8	1	7	4
5	6	7	3	2	4	9	1	8
4	8	2	6	1	9	7	3	5
9	3	1	8	7	5	4	2	6

93

5	6	1	2	4	7	8	3	9
7	8	2	6	9	3	1	5	4
9	4	3	8	1	5	7	2	6
2	3	4	9	6	1	5	8	7
6	5	7	4	3	8	2	9	1
8	1	9	7	5	2	6	4	3
3	7	6	5	8	4	9	1	2
1	9	5	3	2	6	4	7	8
4	2	8	1	7	9	3	6	5

94

9	3	1	6	2	8	5	7	4
4	5	6	1	3	7	2	8	9
8	7	2	5	4	9	6	3	1
3	1	4	2	5	6	7	9	8
6	9	8	4	7	3	1	2	5
5	2	7	9	8	1	4	6	3
1	4	9	8	6	2	3	5	7
7	6	5	3	9	4	8	1	2
2	8	3	7	1	5	9	4	6

95

4	2	7	5	1	3	8	9	6
1	9	3	6	7	8	5	2	4
5	6	8	4	9	2	7	1	3
2	3	4	9	6	5	1	7	8
9	5	1	3	8	7	6	4	2
7	8	6	2	4	1	9	3	5
3	1	2	7	5	6	4	8	9
8	4	5	1	2	9	3	6	7
6	7	9	8	3	4	2	5	1

96

6	1	7	5	2	8	3	9	4
5	3	8	6	9	4	2	7	1
9	4	2	7	1	3	5	6	8
4	8	9	2	5	7	6	1	3
3	5	6	9	4	1	7	8	2
2	7	1	8	3	6	4	5	9
8	6	3	4	7	9	1	2	5
7	2	4	1	8	5	9	3	6
1	9	5	3	6	2	8	4	7

97

3	8	5	4	9	1	6	7	2
1	6	7	3	5	2	9	4	8
2	4	9	7	8	6	1	5	3
4	9	1	5	3	7	8	2	6
5	2	3	1	6	8	4	9	7
8	7	6	2	4	9	3	1	5
9	3	2	6	7	4	5	8	1
7	5	8	9	1	3	2	6	4
6	1	4	8	2	5	7	3	9

98

2	4	6	5	1	7	3	9	8
1	3	5	9	2	8	6	7	4
7	9	8	4	6	3	2	1	5
5	8	3	7	4	1	9	2	6
9	6	2	3	8	5	7	4	1
4	7	1	6	9	2	5	8	3
6	1	4	2	5	9	8	3	7
8	2	7	1	3	6	4	5	9
3	5	9	8	7	4	1	6	2

99

9	3	1	7	4	8	6	2	5
5	8	6	9	2	1	4	3	7
4	2	7	5	6	3	8	1	9
8	1	3	6	5	4	7	9	2
7	6	9	8	1	2	3	5	4
2	5	4	3	7	9	1	6	8
3	9	2	1	8	7	5	4	6
1	7	5	4	9	6	2	8	3
6	4	8	2	3	5	9	7	1

100

3	9	8	2	6	5	4	7	1
6	7	1	4	8	3	9	5	2
2	5	4	1	9	7	8	6	3
4	1	3	8	2	6	7	9	5
7	2	9	3	5	4	6	1	8
8	6	5	7	1	9	2	3	4
5	8	7	9	4	1	3	2	6
9	4	6	5	3	2	1	8	7
1	3	2	6	7	8	5	4	9

101

9	1	5	8	4	3	2	6	7
6	8	2	9	5	7	4	1	3
3	4	7	6	1	2	8	9	5
4	9	3	1	2	8	7	5	6
8	7	1	4	6	5	9	3	2
5	2	6	3	7	9	1	4	8
2	3	8	5	9	1	6	7	4
1	5	4	7	8	6	3	2	9
7	6	9	2	3	4	5	8	1

102

1	6	5	2	8	3	9	7	4
4	8	9	5	6	7	1	2	3
3	2	7	4	9	1	8	5	6
2	4	6	9	3	5	7	1	8
7	9	3	8	1	6	2	4	5
8	5	1	7	4	2	3	6	9
9	1	2	6	5	8	4	3	7
5	3	4	1	7	9	6	8	2
6	7	8	3	2	4	5	9	1

103

7	2	8	3	4	5	9	1	6
6	5	1	2	7	9	4	8	3
3	9	4	6	1	8	5	2	7
1	3	9	7	2	6	8	4	5
2	7	5	4	8	1	6	3	9
4	8	6	5	9	3	2	7	1
5	1	7	8	6	2	3	9	4
9	6	2	1	3	4	7	5	8
8	4	3	9	5	7	1	6	2

104

7	8	2	3	6	4	5	9	1
4	6	9	2	5	1	7	8	3
3	1	5	7	9	8	2	4	6
5	9	4	8	7	3	6	1	2
6	3	8	9	1	2	4	7	5
2	7	1	6	4	5	9	3	8
9	5	7	1	3	6	8	2	4
1	2	6	4	8	9	3	5	7
8	4	3	5	2	7	1	6	9

105

1	2	3	8	5	9	7	4	6
9	7	4	3	1	6	2	5	8
8	5	6	4	7	2	9	3	1
7	1	2	9	4	3	8	6	5
5	6	8	7	2	1	4	9	3
3	4	9	5	6	8	1	7	2
6	8	7	1	3	4	5	2	9
2	9	5	6	8	7	3	1	4
4	3	1	2	9	5	6	8	7

106

2	4	5	6	9	3	1	7	8
1	9	8	2	4	7	5	6	3
3	7	6	8	5	1	4	2	9
5	1	7	9	2	4	3	8	6
9	3	2	1	6	8	7	5	4
6	8	4	7	3	5	2	9	1
7	2	9	4	1	6	8	3	5
8	5	1	3	7	9	6	4	2
4	6	3	5	8	2	9	1	7

107

8	6	2	5	4	1	3	7	9
3	7	1	8	9	6	5	4	2
5	4	9	7	3	2	8	1	6
6	9	3	1	5	7	4	2	8
1	2	5	9	8	4	6	3	7
7	8	4	6	2	3	1	9	5
4	5	8	2	1	9	7	6	3
2	3	7	4	6	5	9	8	1
9	1	6	3	7	8	2	5	4

108

4	6	3	7	1	8	9	5	2
2	5	9	3	4	6	1	7	8
1	8	7	5	2	9	4	3	6
6	9	2	8	7	3	5	1	4
7	1	4	6	5	2	8	9	3
5	3	8	4	9	1	2	6	7
9	7	6	2	8	5	3	4	1
3	2	1	9	6	4	7	8	5
8	4	5	1	3	7	6	2	9

109

6	7	2	5	4	8	3	1	9
5	4	1	6	9	3	8	7	2
8	9	3	2	7	1	6	4	5
3	2	6	4	8	9	7	5	1
4	8	7	1	6	5	9	2	3
9	1	5	7	3	2	4	8	6
7	5	4	3	1	6	2	9	8
1	3	8	9	2	7	5	6	4
2	6	9	8	5	4	1	3	7

110

4	2	8	9	1	5	6	7	3
5	9	6	3	4	7	8	1	2
7	1	3	8	6	2	9	4	5
9	8	7	6	5	4	2	3	1
6	5	2	1	7	3	4	8	9
1	3	4	2	9	8	7	5	6
8	4	9	5	3	6	1	2	7
3	7	1	4	2	9	5	6	8
2	6	5	7	8	1	3	9	4

111

5	1	3	2	4	7	8	6	9
9	8	7	1	6	5	3	2	4
6	2	4	9	8	3	7	5	1
1	6	9	5	2	8	4	3	7
7	4	5	6	3	9	2	1	8
8	3	2	7	1	4	6	9	5
4	9	8	3	5	2	1	7	6
2	5	6	8	7	1	9	4	3
3	7	1	4	9	6	5	8	2

112

4	1	7	3	5	9	8	2	6
8	9	5	2	1	6	7	3	4
3	2	6	7	8	4	9	5	1
2	3	4	1	7	8	6	9	5
5	7	1	6	9	3	4	8	2
9	6	8	4	2	5	3	1	7
7	8	9	5	4	2	1	6	3
6	4	2	9	3	1	5	7	8
1	5	3	8	6	7	2	4	9

113

5	1	4	2	9	6	3	8	7
2	9	6	8	3	7	4	5	1
8	3	7	5	4	1	2	9	6
3	8	2	1	5	4	7	6	9
4	6	1	9	7	3	5	2	8
7	5	9	6	2	8	1	3	4
9	7	5	4	8	2	6	1	3
1	2	3	7	6	9	8	4	5
6	4	8	3	1	5	9	7	2

114

6	5	1	3	8	7	9	4	2
4	3	7	5	9	2	8	1	6
8	2	9	1	4	6	7	3	5
9	4	2	7	1	8	6	5	3
1	7	3	4	6	5	2	9	8
5	8	6	9	2	3	4	7	1
3	6	5	8	7	9	1	2	4
7	1	8	2	5	4	3	6	9
2	9	4	6	3	1	5	8	7

115

7	8	3	9	6	1	4	5	2
9	2	5	3	8	4	1	7	6
4	1	6	5	2	7	8	3	9
1	3	4	6	7	5	2	9	8
2	7	8	1	3	9	5	6	4
5	6	9	8	4	2	3	1	7
6	4	2	7	1	3	9	8	5
8	5	1	2	9	6	7	4	3
3	9	7	4	5	8	6	2	1

116

9	7	3	8	4	6	5	1	2
6	2	5	9	7	1	8	4	3
1	8	4	3	2	5	7	6	9
7	3	2	4	8	9	6	5	1
5	4	1	6	3	2	9	8	7
8	6	9	1	5	7	3	2	4
4	5	6	2	9	3	1	7	8
3	1	8	7	6	4	2	9	5
2	9	7	5	1	8	4	3	6

117

9	8	5	2	3	6	4	1	7
3	4	2	7	1	5	6	9	8
1	6	7	4	8	9	2	3	5
7	5	4	8	6	3	9	2	1
2	9	1	5	4	7	3	8	6
8	3	6	9	2	1	5	7	4
6	1	8	3	9	4	7	5	2
5	2	9	6	7	8	1	4	3
4	7	3	1	5	2	8	6	9

118

1	4	7	8	2	9	6	3	5
9	2	5	3	4	6	8	1	7
6	8	3	1	7	5	2	4	9
7	1	2	5	8	4	9	6	3
5	6	9	2	1	3	7	8	4
4	3	8	9	6	7	5	2	1
8	5	6	7	3	1	4	9	2
2	7	1	4	9	8	3	5	6
3	9	4	6	5	2	1	7	8

119

7	8	9	4	6	2	3	5	1
5	4	1	7	9	3	8	2	6
6	2	3	5	8	1	7	9	4
9	5	6	2	7	4	1	3	8
1	7	8	6	3	9	5	4	2
2	3	4	1	5	8	9	6	7
4	6	5	9	1	7	2	8	3
8	9	7	3	2	6	4	1	5
3	1	2	8	4	5	6	7	9

120

3	4	1	9	7	6	5	2	8
8	5	6	1	2	4	9	7	3
2	9	7	8	5	3	6	4	1
9	8	3	5	1	7	2	6	4
1	7	5	4	6	2	3	8	9
4	6	2	3	8	9	7	1	5
6	3	8	7	9	1	4	5	2
7	1	4	2	3	5	8	9	6
5	2	9	6	4	8	1	3	7

121

3	9	6	8	4	1	5	2	7
2	5	4	9	6	7	1	8	3
8	7	1	2	5	3	4	6	9
7	6	2	5	9	8	3	1	4
4	3	9	6	1	2	8	7	5
5	1	8	3	7	4	2	9	6
1	8	5	7	3	6	9	4	2
9	2	7	4	8	5	6	3	1
6	4	3	1	2	9	7	5	8

122

4	5	3	9	7	8	6	1	2
2	6	7	4	3	1	5	9	8
9	8	1	2	6	5	4	7	3
1	4	2	7	8	3	9	6	5
7	9	6	1	5	2	8	3	4
5	3	8	6	4	9	7	2	1
6	2	9	5	1	4	3	8	7
8	7	4	3	2	6	1	5	9
3	1	5	8	9	7	2	4	6

123

5	2	9	7	1	6	3	8	4
8	3	1	4	2	5	6	9	7
7	6	4	9	8	3	2	5	1
3	8	7	6	4	2	5	1	9
6	4	2	1	5	9	8	7	3
1	9	5	3	7	8	4	2	6
4	5	3	8	9	1	7	6	2
2	1	6	5	3	7	9	4	8
9	7	8	2	6	4	1	3	5

124

6	7	9	2	3	5	4	8	1
5	2	3	8	4	1	7	6	9
4	8	1	9	7	6	3	5	2
2	9	7	1	6	4	5	3	8
3	1	4	7	5	8	9	2	6
8	5	6	3	9	2	1	4	7
7	6	2	4	1	3	8	9	5
9	4	8	5	2	7	6	1	3
1	3	5	6	8	9	2	7	4

125

4	8	2	5	6	9	7	3	1
7	5	6	2	1	3	9	8	4
3	1	9	8	7	4	6	2	5
2	4	5	1	9	8	3	7	6
9	3	8	6	4	7	1	5	2
1	6	7	3	5	2	4	9	8
6	2	1	7	3	5	8	4	9
5	9	3	4	8	1	2	6	7
8	7	4	9	2	6	5	1	3

126

9	5	1	4	7	3	2	6	8
4	6	7	2	5	8	1	3	9
2	3	8	6	1	9	5	7	4
8	7	4	9	3	5	6	1	2
1	2	5	8	4	6	7	9	3
6	9	3	7	2	1	8	4	5
5	4	9	1	6	2	3	8	7
3	8	6	5	9	7	4	2	1
7	1	2	3	8	4	9	5	6

127

4	5	8	1	2	6	3	9	7
7	9	6	4	5	3	1	8	2
1	3	2	9	8	7	4	5	6
2	6	1	5	9	8	7	3	4
8	7	5	6	3	4	9	2	1
3	4	9	2	7	1	8	6	5
6	1	3	8	4	5	2	7	9
5	2	7	3	1	9	6	4	8
9	8	4	7	6	2	5	1	3

128

1	7	6	5	9	4	3	8	2
2	8	3	1	7	6	5	9	4
5	4	9	2	3	8	7	6	1
7	6	5	4	1	3	9	2	8
9	3	8	7	6	2	4	1	5
4	2	1	9	8	5	6	3	7
8	1	4	6	5	9	2	7	3
6	5	7	3	2	1	8	4	9
3	9	2	8	4	7	1	5	6

129

9	6	8	1	3	2	4	5	7
5	1	3	9	7	4	2	6	8
7	4	2	5	6	8	9	1	3
2	9	4	3	8	6	5	7	1
6	5	1	7	2	9	8	3	4
3	8	7	4	1	5	6	9	2
4	7	6	2	5	3	1	8	9
1	2	5	8	9	7	3	4	6
8	3	9	6	4	1	7	2	5

130

2	1	7	3	4	6	9	8	5
9	4	3	2	5	8	1	6	7
8	5	6	9	7	1	2	3	4
7	9	4	8	6	5	3	2	1
5	8	1	4	2	3	6	7	9
3	6	2	7	1	9	4	5	8
1	2	5	6	9	7	8	4	3
6	7	8	1	3	4	5	9	2
4	3	9	5	8	2	7	1	6

131

4	1	2	6	9	7	8	5	3
8	3	6	5	4	1	2	7	9
5	9	7	2	8	3	4	1	6
2	8	9	7	1	5	3	6	4
1	4	3	8	6	9	5	2	7
6	7	5	4	3	2	1	9	8
3	6	1	9	2	8	7	4	5
7	2	4	3	5	6	9	8	1
9	5	8	1	7	4	6	3	2

132

6	7	9	5	1	4	8	3	2
8	3	5	2	6	9	7	1	4
2	4	1	7	8	3	9	5	6
7	9	3	4	5	8	2	6	1
5	8	2	6	7	1	3	4	9
4	1	6	3	9	2	5	8	7
3	6	4	9	2	5	1	7	8
1	2	7	8	3	6	4	9	5
9	5	8	1	4	7	6	2	3

133

4	1	6	7	9	2	5	3	8
7	9	8	5	3	4	2	6	1
2	3	5	6	8	1	9	7	4
3	7	4	2	5	8	1	9	6
5	8	1	9	7	6	4	2	3
9	6	2	1	4	3	7	8	5
6	5	7	8	1	9	3	4	2
8	4	9	3	2	5	6	1	7
1	2	3	4	6	7	8	5	9

134

8	4	9	3	5	2	7	1	6
2	6	5	7	9	1	3	4	8
3	7	1	4	6	8	9	2	5
9	3	7	1	8	4	5	6	2
5	2	8	9	7	6	4	3	1
6	1	4	5	2	3	8	9	7
4	5	2	6	3	7	1	8	9
7	8	3	2	1	9	6	5	4
1	9	6	8	4	5	2	7	3

135

7	5	2	8	6	3	9	1	4
9	8	1	4	5	2	6	7	3
3	6	4	9	1	7	2	8	5
8	7	9	6	2	4	3	5	1
6	1	5	3	9	8	7	4	2
4	2	3	5	7	1	8	9	6
2	3	8	7	4	5	1	6	9
1	4	6	2	8	9	5	3	7
5	9	7	1	3	6	4	2	8

136

4	6	2	5	9	7	1	3	8
1	3	9	6	8	2	7	4	5
8	7	5	3	4	1	9	6	2
9	2	3	7	6	4	8	5	1
5	1	8	2	3	9	6	7	4
6	4	7	8	1	5	2	9	3
7	9	1	4	2	3	5	8	6
3	5	6	1	7	8	4	2	9
2	8	4	9	5	6	3	1	7

137

6	5	7	3	8	1	9	4	2
8	9	2	7	4	6	5	3	1
3	1	4	5	9	2	8	6	7
2	3	6	4	5	9	1	7	8
1	8	9	6	2	7	4	5	3
7	4	5	1	3	8	2	9	6
9	7	1	8	6	4	3	2	5
5	2	8	9	7	3	6	1	4
4	6	3	2	1	5	7	8	9

138

7	2	9	1	8	5	4	3	6
6	3	1	2	9	4	7	8	5
5	8	4	7	6	3	2	9	1
9	4	2	8	5	6	3	1	7
8	7	3	4	2	1	6	5	9
1	5	6	9	3	7	8	2	4
4	9	8	5	7	2	1	6	3
3	1	5	6	4	8	9	7	2
2	6	7	3	1	9	5	4	8

139

5	8	2	3	7	6	9	4	1
3	1	7	8	4	9	2	6	5
9	6	4	1	2	5	8	3	7
8	2	1	5	9	3	6	7	4
6	7	9	2	1	4	5	8	3
4	3	5	6	8	7	1	2	9
7	9	8	4	6	1	3	5	2
1	5	6	7	3	2	4	9	8
2	4	3	9	5	8	7	1	6

140

8	2	3	6	1	5	9	7	4
5	4	9	8	7	2	3	6	1
7	1	6	4	3	9	5	2	8
2	3	1	7	9	6	8	4	5
6	8	7	5	4	3	2	1	9
4	9	5	2	8	1	6	3	7
3	5	8	1	2	4	7	9	6
9	6	4	3	5	7	1	8	2
1	7	2	9	6	8	4	5	3

141

8	7	2	4	6	1	5	9	3
9	4	3	2	8	5	1	7	6
1	6	5	7	3	9	4	8	2
2	9	8	5	1	4	6	3	7
6	3	4	8	7	2	9	1	5
5	1	7	6	9	3	8	2	4
7	8	1	3	5	6	2	4	9
3	2	6	9	4	8	7	5	1
4	5	9	1	2	7	3	6	8

142

5	7	9	1	3	6	2	4	8
1	6	3	2	4	8	9	5	7
8	4	2	9	7	5	1	3	6
4	3	8	7	9	2	6	1	5
6	2	5	3	8	1	4	7	9
7	9	1	5	6	4	8	2	3
9	8	7	4	2	3	5	6	1
3	1	4	6	5	9	7	8	2
2	5	6	8	1	7	3	9	4

143

9	7	2	6	1	8	3	5	4
1	4	8	5	9	3	2	7	6
6	3	5	2	7	4	8	1	9
8	1	4	9	6	7	5	2	3
7	2	9	3	8	5	6	4	1
5	6	3	1	4	2	9	8	7
3	5	7	4	2	6	1	9	8
4	9	6	8	5	1	7	3	2
2	8	1	7	3	9	4	6	5

144

4	9	3	5	7	2	1	6	8
8	6	5	1	4	9	3	7	2
1	2	7	8	3	6	5	9	4
5	4	2	9	8	3	7	1	6
6	7	1	4	2	5	8	3	9
3	8	9	7	6	1	4	2	5
7	3	6	2	5	8	9	4	1
9	5	4	6	1	7	2	8	3
2	1	8	3	9	4	6	5	7

145

1	9	6	5	4	7	2	3	8
5	2	7	9	3	8	1	4	6
3	4	8	1	2	6	7	9	5
9	3	4	2	8	5	6	1	7
2	8	1	6	7	9	3	5	4
7	6	5	3	1	4	9	8	2
4	5	2	7	9	1	8	6	3
6	1	3	8	5	2	4	7	9
8	7	9	4	6	3	5	2	1

146

3	4	7	2	1	5	9	8	6
9	1	8	6	7	3	5	2	4
5	6	2	4	9	8	7	3	1
1	7	9	3	4	2	6	5	8
2	8	6	9	5	7	1	4	3
4	3	5	8	6	1	2	7	9
7	9	4	5	3	6	8	1	2
6	2	1	7	8	4	3	9	5
8	5	3	1	2	9	4	6	7

147

6	9	7	3	4	5	8	2	1
5	1	3	9	8	2	6	4	7
8	4	2	6	1	7	9	3	5
1	3	8	2	6	4	7	5	9
4	2	6	7	5	9	3	1	8
9	7	5	8	3	1	4	6	2
7	8	4	1	2	6	5	9	3
3	6	1	5	9	8	2	7	4
2	5	9	4	7	3	1	8	6

148

1	3	9	5	7	4	2	6	8
2	5	4	6	1	8	9	7	3
7	6	8	3	9	2	4	1	5
9	2	7	1	3	5	8	4	6
8	1	5	9	4	6	3	2	7
6	4	3	2	8	7	5	9	1
3	9	6	4	5	1	7	8	2
4	7	1	8	2	3	6	5	9
5	8	2	7	6	9	1	3	4

149

8	9	6	2	7	3	5	1	4
4	1	7	6	8	5	9	3	2
2	3	5	9	4	1	7	8	6
9	4	1	8	6	7	2	5	3
5	2	3	1	9	4	8	6	7
6	7	8	5	3	2	4	9	1
7	6	4	3	5	9	1	2	8
1	8	9	4	2	6	3	7	5
3	5	2	7	1	8	6	4	9

150

2	4	7	9	5	8	6	3	1
5	8	6	3	7	1	2	4	9
9	1	3	4	6	2	8	7	5
8	5	1	2	9	7	3	6	4
4	3	2	6	8	5	1	9	7
6	7	9	1	3	4	5	8	2
1	2	8	7	4	3	9	5	6
7	9	5	8	2	6	4	1	3
3	6	4	5	1	9	7	2	8

151

2	9	6	8	3	5	7	1	4
8	7	1	9	6	4	3	5	2
5	4	3	2	1	7	8	6	9
3	8	9	6	4	1	2	7	5
4	2	7	3	5	8	1	9	6
1	6	5	7	2	9	4	3	8
6	1	4	5	8	3	9	2	7
9	3	2	4	7	6	5	8	1
7	5	8	1	9	2	6	4	3

152

5	2	4	6	1	7	9	3	8
8	6	3	5	4	9	7	2	1
7	9	1	8	2	3	6	4	5
9	4	7	1	8	6	3	5	2
2	1	6	7	3	5	8	9	4
3	5	8	4	9	2	1	6	7
6	7	9	2	5	8	4	1	3
4	3	2	9	7	1	5	8	6
1	8	5	3	6	4	2	7	9

153

4	2	3	5	9	8	7	1	6
9	8	1	6	2	7	4	5	3
5	7	6	4	1	3	2	9	8
2	6	8	7	4	1	5	3	9
1	9	5	3	8	2	6	7	4
7	3	4	9	5	6	8	2	1
3	4	7	2	6	9	1	8	5
8	5	2	1	3	4	9	6	7
6	1	9	8	7	5	3	4	2

154

7	3	4	5	8	2	9	6	1
5	1	6	4	9	7	8	2	3
8	9	2	3	1	6	5	4	7
1	6	9	8	7	5	2	3	4
2	8	3	9	4	1	7	5	6
4	5	7	2	6	3	1	9	8
6	7	5	1	3	9	4	8	2
9	4	1	6	2	8	3	7	5
3	2	8	7	5	4	6	1	9

155

3	7	9	6	1	5	4	2	8
6	8	4	3	2	9	7	1	5
5	2	1	4	7	8	6	3	9
8	9	7	2	4	1	3	5	6
1	5	3	7	9	6	2	8	4
4	6	2	8	5	3	1	9	7
9	4	8	1	3	7	5	6	2
2	3	6	5	8	4	9	7	1
7	1	5	9	6	2	8	4	3

156

5	6	8	3	4	7	2	9	1
7	3	1	6	2	9	8	5	4
4	2	9	8	1	5	3	7	6
8	5	6	2	7	3	1	4	9
2	1	7	4	9	8	5	6	3
9	4	3	5	6	1	7	2	8
1	9	5	7	8	4	6	3	2
6	7	4	1	3	2	9	8	5
3	8	2	9	5	6	4	1	7

157

3	6	8	4	2	9	1	7	5
9	4	5	6	7	1	2	8	3
7	1	2	8	5	3	6	9	4
5	7	4	9	1	8	3	2	6
1	9	6	7	3	2	5	4	8
8	2	3	5	4	6	7	1	9
6	5	7	2	8	4	9	3	1
4	3	9	1	6	7	8	5	2
2	8	1	3	9	5	4	6	7

158

5	4	7	2	6	9	1	3	8
9	8	2	7	3	1	6	4	5
3	1	6	5	4	8	9	2	7
2	6	5	4	9	7	3	8	1
8	7	9	6	1	3	4	5	2
1	3	4	8	5	2	7	6	9
6	9	8	3	7	5	2	1	4
4	2	1	9	8	6	5	7	3
7	5	3	1	2	4	8	9	6

159

9	4	6	5	1	2	3	7	8
2	8	5	3	9	7	6	1	4
1	3	7	6	8	4	9	2	5
5	7	1	9	4	6	2	8	3
4	6	9	8	2	3	7	5	1
8	2	3	1	7	5	4	6	9
7	1	8	2	3	9	5	4	6
3	5	2	4	6	8	1	9	7
6	9	4	7	5	1	8	3	2

160

5	4	6	7	3	2	1	8	9
8	2	9	4	5	1	6	3	7
3	7	1	9	6	8	4	2	5
9	5	8	3	4	6	2	7	1
2	3	4	5	1	7	8	9	6
6	1	7	8	2	9	5	4	3
7	6	2	1	8	3	9	5	4
4	8	3	6	9	5	7	1	2
1	9	5	2	7	4	3	6	8

161

7	9	4	3	1	2	8	6	5
3	5	8	6	9	4	7	1	2
1	6	2	7	5	8	4	9	3
6	1	3	4	7	9	2	5	8
4	2	7	1	8	5	9	3	6
9	8	5	2	6	3	1	7	4
2	3	1	5	4	7	6	8	9
5	7	9	8	2	6	3	4	1
8	4	6	9	3	1	5	2	7

162

9	6	3	4	8	2	1	5	7
2	5	1	3	9	7	6	4	8
7	4	8	5	1	6	3	9	2
3	2	9	1	6	5	8	7	4
5	1	4	7	2	8	9	6	3
8	7	6	9	3	4	5	2	1
4	8	2	6	5	3	7	1	9
1	3	5	2	7	9	4	8	6
6	9	7	8	4	1	2	3	5

163

7	8	2	6	5	4	1	3	9
4	5	6	1	3	9	8	2	7
9	3	1	7	8	2	6	4	5
6	7	3	8	9	1	2	5	4
2	4	5	3	6	7	9	1	8
1	9	8	4	2	5	7	6	3
8	1	4	2	7	3	5	9	6
5	2	7	9	4	6	3	8	1
3	6	9	5	1	8	4	7	2

164

3	9	6	7	2	5	8	4	1
5	1	2	4	9	8	3	7	6
8	4	7	3	6	1	2	5	9
9	5	8	6	3	7	4	1	2
6	2	3	5	1	4	9	8	7
4	7	1	2	8	9	6	3	5
1	6	4	9	7	3	5	2	8
7	3	9	8	5	2	1	6	4
2	8	5	1	4	6	7	9	3

165

3	1	6	5	2	4	8	7	9
4	2	8	9	3	7	6	1	5
5	9	7	8	6	1	3	2	4
9	6	4	3	8	2	1	5	7
2	7	1	4	5	6	9	8	3
8	5	3	7	1	9	2	4	6
7	8	5	2	9	3	4	6	1
1	4	9	6	7	8	5	3	2
6	3	2	1	4	5	7	9	8

166

1	7	6	5	8	9	2	4	3
2	3	5	4	6	1	9	7	8
9	8	4	3	2	7	5	6	1
6	2	7	8	4	3	1	9	5
5	1	8	7	9	6	4	3	2
3	4	9	2	1	5	7	8	6
4	5	3	6	7	2	8	1	9
7	9	2	1	3	8	6	5	4
8	6	1	9	5	4	3	2	7

167

9	1	7	8	3	2	5	6	4
2	5	6	4	7	1	9	8	3
3	8	4	5	6	9	1	7	2
6	2	8	7	5	3	4	9	1
5	7	9	6	1	4	3	2	8
4	3	1	9	2	8	6	5	7
1	9	2	3	8	6	7	4	5
7	6	3	2	4	5	8	1	9
8	4	5	1	9	7	2	3	6

168

1	8	5	4	3	7	6	9	2
9	6	2	8	5	1	3	4	7
3	4	7	2	9	6	5	1	8
8	9	3	7	4	5	2	6	1
5	1	6	9	8	2	4	7	3
7	2	4	1	6	3	9	8	5
2	3	9	6	7	8	1	5	4
6	7	1	5	2	4	8	3	9
4	5	8	3	1	9	7	2	6

169

2	4	3	5	8	6	9	1	7
1	7	5	2	4	9	3	6	8
6	8	9	7	3	1	4	5	2
9	1	8	6	2	4	7	3	5
4	2	7	8	5	3	6	9	1
5	3	6	1	9	7	2	8	4
7	5	4	3	6	8	1	2	9
3	9	2	4	1	5	8	7	6
8	6	1	9	7	2	5	4	3

170

8	2	6	7	4	5	9	1	3
5	7	3	2	9	1	4	8	6
9	1	4	8	3	6	2	7	5
2	8	9	5	7	3	1	6	4
3	6	7	1	8	4	5	9	2
4	5	1	6	2	9	8	3	7
7	3	2	4	1	8	6	5	9
1	4	5	9	6	7	3	2	8
6	9	8	3	5	2	7	4	1

171

6	2	3	5	7	1	8	4	9
5	1	9	3	8	4	7	2	6
7	8	4	2	6	9	5	1	3
9	3	8	1	5	7	4	6	2
2	6	1	9	4	8	3	5	7
4	7	5	6	2	3	9	8	1
8	9	6	4	3	2	1	7	5
3	4	2	7	1	5	6	9	8
1	5	7	8	9	6	2	3	4

172

6	5	2	8	3	9	7	1	4
3	7	8	2	1	4	5	6	9
4	9	1	5	7	6	3	8	2
1	6	5	7	8	2	9	4	3
8	4	9	6	5	3	2	7	1
2	3	7	4	9	1	6	5	8
7	8	3	9	4	5	1	2	6
5	1	6	3	2	8	4	9	7
9	2	4	1	6	7	8	3	5

173

7	8	3	1	2	4	6	9	5
6	2	4	7	5	9	1	3	8
9	1	5	8	6	3	7	2	4
2	7	8	3	4	6	5	1	9
3	4	1	5	9	8	2	7	6
5	9	6	2	1	7	8	4	3
8	6	9	4	7	1	3	5	2
4	5	7	6	3	2	9	8	1
1	3	2	9	8	5	4	6	7

174

5	6	4	9	2	1	7	3	8
2	8	9	5	7	3	1	4	6
7	3	1	8	6	4	5	9	2
4	1	7	6	3	8	9	2	5
8	2	3	1	9	5	4	6	7
9	5	6	7	4	2	3	8	1
1	7	2	3	8	9	6	5	4
6	9	8	4	5	7	2	1	3
3	4	5	2	1	6	8	7	9

175

4	8	7	3	5	6	2	9	1
9	2	3	1	7	8	4	6	5
6	5	1	4	2	9	3	7	8
2	6	5	9	4	7	8	1	3
3	9	8	5	1	2	7	4	6
1	7	4	6	8	3	5	2	9
7	1	6	8	3	4	9	5	2
5	3	2	7	9	1	6	8	4
8	4	9	2	6	5	1	3	7

176

4	8	6	3	2	1	7	5	9
1	5	3	4	9	7	8	2	6
2	9	7	5	6	8	1	3	4
3	7	9	8	1	4	5	6	2
5	4	8	6	7	2	3	9	1
6	1	2	9	5	3	4	7	8
7	6	5	1	4	9	2	8	3
9	3	1	2	8	5	6	4	7
8	2	4	7	3	6	9	1	5

177

9	6	7	8	2	1	5	4	3
8	2	3	6	5	4	7	9	1
5	1	4	7	9	3	6	2	8
3	4	9	5	1	6	8	7	2
6	7	1	9	8	2	3	5	4
2	8	5	4	3	7	1	6	9
1	9	2	3	6	5	4	8	7
4	5	8	1	7	9	2	3	6
7	3	6	2	4	8	9	1	5

178

8	3	7	5	2	6	9	1	4
9	5	1	7	8	4	3	2	6
6	2	4	9	1	3	7	8	5
7	4	3	8	9	1	6	5	2
5	8	6	2	4	7	1	9	3
2	1	9	3	6	5	8	4	7
3	7	2	1	5	8	4	6	9
1	6	5	4	7	9	2	3	8
4	9	8	6	3	2	5	7	1

179

1	7	5	6	8	2	9	4	3
4	9	3	7	1	5	8	6	2
8	2	6	3	4	9	7	1	5
7	8	4	5	3	6	2	9	1
9	5	1	8	2	4	6	3	7
6	3	2	1	9	7	5	8	4
3	1	7	2	6	8	4	5	9
5	6	9	4	7	1	3	2	8
2	4	8	9	5	3	1	7	6

180

7	4	6	9	8	2	3	1	5
8	2	3	4	5	1	6	7	9
1	9	5	3	6	7	8	4	2
2	3	7	5	4	6	9	8	1
4	5	9	2	1	8	7	6	3
6	1	8	7	9	3	2	5	4
9	6	4	8	3	5	1	2	7
3	8	2	1	7	4	5	9	6
5	7	1	6	2	9	4	3	8

181

8	6	2	1	9	4	7	3	5
1	7	4	2	3	5	8	6	9
3	9	5	6	8	7	4	2	1
6	4	8	9	7	2	1	5	3
7	2	1	8	5	3	6	9	4
9	5	3	4	6	1	2	7	8
5	8	7	3	4	6	9	1	2
4	1	6	5	2	9	3	8	7
2	3	9	7	1	8	5	4	6

182

6	5	4	7	3	2	1	8	9
1	9	3	4	6	8	7	5	2
2	7	8	1	9	5	6	3	4
5	6	9	2	8	7	4	1	3
3	8	2	9	1	4	5	7	6
4	1	7	6	5	3	9	2	8
8	2	6	5	4	1	3	9	7
9	3	5	8	7	6	2	4	1
7	4	1	3	2	9	8	6	5

183

1	7	3	5	6	9	2	4	8
2	8	4	3	1	7	6	9	5
6	5	9	8	2	4	1	7	3
4	2	7	9	3	6	8	5	1
3	9	5	2	8	1	7	6	4
8	6	1	4	7	5	3	2	9
5	1	8	7	9	2	4	3	6
7	4	6	1	5	3	9	8	2
9	3	2	6	4	8	5	1	7

184

2	8	1	4	5	6	7	3	9
7	5	9	1	8	3	6	4	2
4	6	3	2	7	9	8	1	5
3	9	2	8	6	7	4	5	1
5	1	7	9	3	4	2	8	6
8	4	6	5	2	1	3	9	7
6	3	4	7	1	5	9	2	8
1	7	8	3	9	2	5	6	4
9	2	5	6	4	8	1	7	3

185

1	6	2	8	9	5	7	3	4
3	8	4	6	1	7	2	9	5
5	9	7	2	3	4	1	6	8
7	3	8	4	2	6	9	5	1
6	1	5	3	7	9	4	8	2
2	4	9	1	5	8	3	7	6
4	7	1	5	8	3	6	2	9
9	5	6	7	4	2	8	1	3
8	2	3	9	6	1	5	4	7

186

6	3	5	9	7	2	8	1	4
9	2	8	6	1	4	7	5	3
7	1	4	5	3	8	2	9	6
1	8	9	3	4	5	6	7	2
3	7	6	1	2	9	4	8	5
5	4	2	7	8	6	1	3	9
4	6	3	8	5	7	9	2	1
2	5	7	4	9	1	3	6	8
8	9	1	2	6	3	5	4	7

187

2	3	8	1	9	6	7	4	5
6	5	7	4	8	2	1	3	9
4	1	9	7	3	5	8	2	6
8	9	3	5	4	7	2	6	1
1	2	4	9	6	8	3	5	7
5	7	6	3	2	1	9	8	4
3	8	1	6	7	4	5	9	2
7	4	2	8	5	9	6	1	3
9	6	5	2	1	3	4	7	8

188

2	1	4	6	3	9	8	5	7
3	8	9	1	5	7	4	6	2
6	5	7	8	4	2	1	3	9
7	6	3	4	2	1	5	9	8
8	4	2	9	6	5	7	1	3
1	9	5	7	8	3	6	2	4
9	2	6	5	7	4	3	8	1
4	3	8	2	1	6	9	7	5
5	7	1	3	9	8	2	4	6

189

1	8	3	4	6	5	7	2	9
6	7	5	1	2	9	4	8	3
9	4	2	7	8	3	1	5	6
7	2	1	9	3	6	5	4	8
5	9	8	2	7	4	3	6	1
3	6	4	5	1	8	2	9	7
4	3	9	8	5	1	6	7	2
8	1	7	6	4	2	9	3	5
2	5	6	3	9	7	8	1	4

190

3	1	4	7	5	9	6	2	8
5	6	8	3	4	2	1	7	9
9	2	7	1	6	8	5	3	4
8	4	5	2	1	6	3	9	7
2	3	9	8	7	5	4	1	6
6	7	1	4	9	3	2	8	5
4	5	2	9	8	1	7	6	3
1	8	6	5	3	7	9	4	2
7	9	3	6	2	4	8	5	1

191

7	8	3	6	2	5	4	1	9
5	4	1	8	9	3	2	6	7
9	2	6	7	1	4	5	3	8
4	7	5	2	8	1	3	9	6
6	9	2	3	4	7	1	8	5
3	1	8	9	5	6	7	4	2
8	6	4	1	7	2	9	5	3
2	5	9	4	3	8	6	7	1
1	3	7	5	6	9	8	2	4

192

8	2	3	1	9	7	6	5	4
4	1	7	8	6	5	2	3	9
5	9	6	3	4	2	8	7	1
9	3	5	7	2	1	4	6	8
6	7	1	4	3	8	9	2	5
2	8	4	9	5	6	7	1	3
1	6	2	5	8	9	3	4	7
3	5	9	2	7	4	1	8	6
7	4	8	6	1	3	5	9	2

193

6	2	3	7	4	1	9	5	8
7	9	5	6	8	2	4	3	1
1	8	4	5	9	3	2	7	6
2	4	8	9	6	7	3	1	5
5	7	1	8	3	4	6	2	9
9	3	6	1	2	5	8	4	7
3	6	7	2	1	8	5	9	4
4	1	9	3	5	6	7	8	2
8	5	2	4	7	9	1	6	3

194

8	4	9	2	1	6	5	3	7
7	2	5	3	4	8	6	9	1
1	3	6	7	9	5	2	4	8
5	8	1	9	7	4	3	6	2
6	9	3	8	5	2	7	1	4
4	7	2	6	3	1	8	5	9
9	6	4	5	2	7	1	8	3
2	1	8	4	6	3	9	7	5
3	5	7	1	8	9	4	2	6

195

8	3	2	1	6	7	5	4	9
1	7	9	3	5	4	6	8	2
4	6	5	8	2	9	1	7	3
7	2	8	5	4	3	9	1	6
9	5	3	7	1	6	8	2	4
6	4	1	2	9	8	7	3	5
2	1	4	9	8	5	3	6	7
3	9	6	4	7	1	2	5	8
5	8	7	6	3	2	4	9	1

196

3	4	6	8	5	7	1	2	9
9	5	7	6	2	1	3	8	4
2	8	1	3	9	4	5	7	6
8	6	3	5	7	9	4	1	2
5	9	4	2	1	8	7	6	3
7	1	2	4	3	6	8	9	5
1	2	9	7	4	3	6	5	8
4	7	8	9	6	5	2	3	1
6	3	5	1	8	2	9	4	7

197

6	9	5	3	7	1	2	8	4
4	8	2	9	6	5	7	1	3
3	1	7	4	2	8	5	9	6
9	3	8	2	5	6	1	4	7
1	7	6	8	4	3	9	2	5
5	2	4	1	9	7	6	3	8
8	5	1	6	3	2	4	7	9
2	6	9	7	8	4	3	5	1
7	4	3	5	1	9	8	6	2

198

1	9	8	7	2	3	6	5	4
2	3	6	1	5	4	7	9	8
5	4	7	8	9	6	1	2	3
4	1	9	3	7	2	8	6	5
8	7	5	4	6	9	3	1	2
6	2	3	5	1	8	9	4	7
7	6	4	9	8	5	2	3	1
9	5	1	2	3	7	4	8	6
3	8	2	6	4	1	5	7	9

199

8	2	7	1	4	6	3	5	9
6	4	3	7	5	9	1	8	2
1	9	5	2	3	8	6	7	4
5	3	9	8	1	7	2	4	6
4	6	2	5	9	3	7	1	8
7	8	1	4	6	2	5	9	3
3	1	4	9	2	5	8	6	7
2	5	8	6	7	4	9	3	1
9	7	6	3	8	1	4	2	5

200

4	3	6	2	1	5	8	7	9
9	8	2	4	3	7	6	5	1
7	5	1	9	8	6	2	4	3
1	7	9	5	2	4	3	6	8
8	6	3	1	7	9	5	2	4
5	2	4	3	6	8	1	9	7
6	9	5	8	4	3	7	1	2
3	1	7	6	9	2	4	8	5
2	4	8	7	5	1	9	3	6

201

5	8	1	9	4	7	3	2	6
7	3	9	2	5	6	1	4	8
4	2	6	8	3	1	7	9	5
1	7	2	3	6	4	5	8	9
8	6	4	1	9	5	2	7	3
9	5	3	7	8	2	6	1	4
6	9	7	4	2	3	8	5	1
3	1	8	5	7	9	4	6	2
2	4	5	6	1	8	9	3	7

202

9	8	5	2	1	6	3	4	7
1	7	4	5	3	8	9	6	2
3	2	6	4	7	9	1	5	8
2	4	8	1	6	3	7	9	5
7	5	9	8	4	2	6	3	1
6	3	1	9	5	7	8	2	4
8	9	3	7	2	5	4	1	6
4	6	2	3	8	1	5	7	9
5	1	7	6	9	4	2	8	3

203

7	3	4	9	2	1	8	5	6
5	6	8	7	3	4	9	2	1
2	1	9	5	8	6	3	7	4
3	4	2	1	9	5	7	6	8
6	7	5	2	4	8	1	3	9
9	8	1	3	6	7	5	4	2
1	5	6	8	7	2	4	9	3
4	9	7	6	1	3	2	8	5
8	2	3	4	5	9	6	1	7

204

3	2	9	6	5	1	7	4	8
4	5	1	8	7	3	6	2	9
7	6	8	4	9	2	3	5	1
5	4	2	9	1	6	8	7	3
6	8	3	2	4	7	1	9	5
1	9	7	3	8	5	4	6	2
9	1	6	7	2	8	5	3	4
8	7	4	5	3	9	2	1	6
2	3	5	1	6	4	9	8	7

205

2	6	7	4	5	1	3	8	9
9	8	3	7	2	6	5	4	1
5	1	4	9	8	3	7	2	6
7	2	6	1	4	5	9	3	8
1	9	5	6	3	8	4	7	2
3	4	8	2	9	7	1	6	5
8	7	9	5	6	4	2	1	3
4	3	2	8	1	9	6	5	7
6	5	1	3	7	2	8	9	4

206

2	6	1	8	3	5	7	9	4
3	5	9	1	7	4	8	2	6
7	4	8	2	9	6	3	1	5
4	8	2	7	6	9	1	5	3
6	1	5	3	4	2	9	8	7
9	7	3	5	8	1	6	4	2
1	9	7	4	5	3	2	6	8
5	3	6	9	2	8	4	7	1
8	2	4	6	1	7	5	3	9

207

6	3	2	4	5	1	7	9	8
5	8	7	2	6	9	3	1	4
9	4	1	3	7	8	5	6	2
1	9	4	8	3	2	6	5	7
7	2	8	6	9	5	1	4	3
3	6	5	7	1	4	8	2	9
2	5	9	1	8	3	4	7	6
8	1	6	9	4	7	2	3	5
4	7	3	5	2	6	9	8	1

208

5	4	6	3	9	2	7	8	1
2	1	7	4	5	8	3	6	9
3	9	8	6	1	7	2	5	4
8	5	9	1	4	3	6	7	2
4	6	1	7	2	5	8	9	3
7	3	2	9	8	6	4	1	5
1	8	3	2	7	9	5	4	6
9	2	5	8	6	4	1	3	7
6	7	4	5	3	1	9	2	8

209

2	5	6	9	3	8	1	4	7
7	8	9	5	1	4	6	2	3
4	1	3	6	7	2	9	8	5
1	3	5	7	8	6	2	9	4
9	6	7	4	2	1	3	5	8
8	2	4	3	5	9	7	1	6
5	7	1	8	9	3	4	6	2
3	4	2	1	6	5	8	7	9
6	9	8	2	4	7	5	3	1

210

5	4	8	3	7	1	2	6	9
9	3	7	8	2	6	5	4	1
2	6	1	4	9	5	7	8	3
3	9	5	1	4	7	6	2	8
7	8	6	2	3	9	4	1	5
4	1	2	6	5	8	3	9	7
8	2	9	5	6	3	1	7	4
1	5	4	7	8	2	9	3	6
6	7	3	9	1	4	8	5	2

211

4	8	9	3	2	6	7	1	5
1	6	7	8	5	4	3	2	9
5	2	3	1	7	9	8	4	6
6	3	1	7	4	2	5	9	8
7	4	5	9	8	3	1	6	2
2	9	8	6	1	5	4	7	3
8	7	6	5	9	1	2	3	4
9	5	2	4	3	7	6	8	1
3	1	4	2	6	8	9	5	7

212

8	4	2	6	3	1	5	7	9
7	6	3	2	5	9	1	8	4
5	9	1	4	7	8	6	2	3
4	8	9	3	2	5	7	6	1
3	7	6	8	1	4	9	5	2
2	1	5	7	9	6	3	4	8
9	2	7	5	4	3	8	1	6
6	3	4	1	8	7	2	9	5
1	5	8	9	6	2	4	3	7

213

6	1	9	2	7	8	4	5	3
2	4	8	6	5	3	7	9	1
3	7	5	1	9	4	6	8	2
9	6	3	5	8	7	2	1	4
5	2	7	4	3	1	9	6	8
1	8	4	9	6	2	3	7	5
7	5	1	3	2	6	8	4	9
4	3	6	8	1	9	5	2	7
8	9	2	7	4	5	1	3	6

214

2	8	4	9	6	1	5	7	3
7	1	6	2	3	5	8	9	4
9	3	5	7	4	8	6	2	1
5	4	9	8	2	3	7	1	6
1	2	7	4	5	6	9	3	8
3	6	8	1	9	7	4	5	2
4	7	3	6	1	9	2	8	5
8	5	2	3	7	4	1	6	9
6	9	1	5	8	2	3	4	7

215

4	7	1	6	9	5	2	3	8
6	3	5	7	8	2	9	4	1
2	9	8	4	3	1	6	5	7
7	6	3	8	1	4	5	9	2
9	1	4	5	2	6	7	8	3
8	5	2	3	7	9	1	6	4
1	2	6	9	4	8	3	7	5
5	8	7	2	6	3	4	1	9
3	4	9	1	5	7	8	2	6

216

9	1	4	3	2	7	5	8	6
6	8	7	5	9	4	2	3	1
3	2	5	8	6	1	9	7	4
1	6	2	7	5	8	4	9	3
5	9	8	2	4	3	1	6	7
7	4	3	9	1	6	8	2	5
4	3	1	6	8	2	7	5	9
2	5	6	4	7	9	3	1	8
8	7	9	1	3	5	6	4	2

217

4	7	1	6	9	8	3	2	5
6	9	2	7	3	5	8	1	4
8	5	3	2	1	4	7	6	9
1	8	7	9	6	2	5	4	3
9	6	4	5	8	3	2	7	1
2	3	5	4	7	1	9	8	6
5	2	9	1	4	7	6	3	8
3	4	6	8	2	9	1	5	7
7	1	8	3	5	6	4	9	2

218

2	6	7	8	1	9	5	3	4
9	8	1	3	5	4	6	2	7
3	4	5	2	7	6	8	9	1
1	2	6	4	9	3	7	8	5
7	3	8	6	2	5	4	1	9
4	5	9	1	8	7	3	6	2
6	7	3	9	4	1	2	5	8
8	1	4	5	6	2	9	7	3
5	9	2	7	3	8	1	4	6

219

3	4	2	9	7	1	6	8	5
6	5	8	4	3	2	9	1	7
7	9	1	5	8	6	2	3	4
9	6	3	7	5	8	4	2	1
4	8	5	1	2	9	3	7	6
2	1	7	6	4	3	5	9	8
8	3	6	2	1	4	7	5	9
1	7	4	3	9	5	8	6	2
5	2	9	8	6	7	1	4	3

220

3	4	7	1	8	9	5	6	2
2	9	5	3	6	4	8	1	7
6	8	1	5	7	2	9	3	4
9	7	6	2	4	8	3	5	1
1	2	8	9	3	5	4	7	6
5	3	4	7	1	6	2	8	9
7	1	2	8	9	3	6	4	5
4	5	3	6	2	7	1	9	8
8	6	9	4	5	1	7	2	3

221

2	1	6	4	5	7	8	3	9
5	9	3	1	6	8	7	4	2
4	8	7	2	3	9	6	5	1
9	5	4	6	7	3	1	2	8
3	6	2	9	8	1	5	7	4
1	7	8	5	2	4	3	9	6
8	2	9	7	1	5	4	6	3
7	4	1	3	9	6	2	8	5
6	3	5	8	4	2	9	1	7

222

2	6	4	7	9	1	3	5	8
3	5	7	6	4	8	1	9	2
9	8	1	5	3	2	6	4	7
8	4	6	9	1	3	7	2	5
5	9	2	4	6	7	8	3	1
7	1	3	2	8	5	9	6	4
6	2	9	1	7	4	5	8	3
1	3	5	8	2	9	4	7	6
4	7	8	3	5	6	2	1	9

223

9	8	4	3	5	7	1	6	2
2	7	3	4	1	6	5	9	8
1	5	6	8	2	9	4	7	3
4	3	5	1	6	2	9	8	7
6	9	2	7	4	8	3	5	1
7	1	8	5	9	3	2	4	6
8	4	9	6	3	1	7	2	5
3	2	7	9	8	5	6	1	4
5	6	1	2	7	4	8	3	9

224

9	5	7	4	3	1	6	2	8
4	6	3	8	2	9	7	5	1
8	2	1	7	6	5	9	4	3
5	1	6	9	4	8	3	7	2
7	4	8	2	1	3	5	6	9
2	3	9	5	7	6	8	1	4
3	9	2	6	5	4	1	8	7
6	8	4	1	9	7	2	3	5
1	7	5	3	8	2	4	9	6

Puzzle 225

2	9	4	8	5	7	1	6	3
1	8	7	6	4	3	2	5	9
3	6	5	9	1	2	4	7	8
8	2	1	7	3	9	5	4	6
9	5	6	2	8	4	7	3	1
7	4	3	5	6	1	8	9	2
6	1	8	3	7	5	9	2	4
5	3	2	4	9	8	6	1	7
4	7	9	1	2	6	3	8	5

Puzzle 226

5	7	1	6	4	3	9	8	2
9	2	6	1	8	5	4	3	7
8	4	3	7	9	2	6	1	5
2	3	7	9	5	8	1	6	4
6	1	8	4	3	7	2	5	9
4	9	5	2	1	6	8	7	3
7	8	9	3	6	4	5	2	1
1	6	2	5	7	9	3	4	8
3	5	4	8	2	1	7	9	6

Puzzle 227

7	2	5	1	9	4	3	8	6
8	9	6	2	3	5	1	4	7
1	4	3	7	8	6	5	2	9
5	8	1	4	2	9	7	6	3
3	7	2	6	5	1	4	9	8
9	6	4	3	7	8	2	1	5
4	5	8	9	1	3	6	7	2
6	3	7	8	4	2	9	5	1
2	1	9	5	6	7	8	3	4

Puzzle 228

4	1	8	5	3	7	2	9	6
9	6	5	1	4	2	7	8	3
3	7	2	6	8	9	5	1	4
5	2	7	4	6	1	9	3	8
6	4	3	9	5	8	1	2	7
1	8	9	7	2	3	6	4	5
2	5	6	3	1	4	8	7	9
7	3	1	8	9	5	4	6	2
8	9	4	2	7	6	3	5	1

Puzzle 229

8	5	9	1	2	3	7	6	4
2	7	3	4	8	6	1	5	9
6	1	4	7	9	5	3	2	8
4	2	5	3	1	9	8	7	6
7	6	8	2	5	4	9	3	1
3	9	1	8	6	7	5	4	2
9	3	7	6	4	8	2	1	5
5	4	2	9	7	1	6	8	3
1	8	6	5	3	2	4	9	7

Puzzle 230

1	9	7	8	2	3	5	4	6
3	2	4	5	9	6	7	1	8
6	8	5	4	1	7	9	3	2
8	5	1	3	7	9	2	6	4
7	6	9	2	4	8	1	5	3
4	3	2	6	5	1	8	9	7
9	1	6	7	3	2	4	8	5
2	4	8	1	6	5	3	7	9
5	7	3	9	8	4	6	2	1

Puzzle 231

1	2	9	5	6	4	3	7	8
5	8	7	2	1	3	4	6	9
3	4	6	7	8	9	5	1	2
2	5	8	4	9	6	7	3	1
9	1	4	3	7	8	2	5	6
7	6	3	1	2	5	9	8	4
4	9	1	6	3	7	8	2	5
8	3	2	9	5	1	6	4	7
6	7	5	8	4	2	1	9	3

Puzzle 232

4	9	1	2	7	6	3	8	5
5	2	7	1	3	8	9	6	4
6	3	8	4	9	5	1	7	2
8	1	9	6	4	7	2	5	3
7	6	2	9	5	3	4	1	8
3	4	5	8	2	1	6	9	7
2	5	3	7	6	9	8	4	1
1	7	6	3	8	4	5	2	9
9	8	4	5	1	2	7	3	6

233

5	2	1	6	7	4	8	9	3
6	9	8	1	5	3	4	2	7
4	3	7	8	9	2	6	5	1
8	5	4	3	2	6	1	7	9
3	7	9	4	1	5	2	8	6
2	1	6	9	8	7	3	4	5
9	8	3	7	4	1	5	6	2
7	6	2	5	3	8	9	1	4
1	4	5	2	6	9	7	3	8

234

7	3	2	9	4	8	1	6	5
4	5	8	2	1	6	7	9	3
6	9	1	7	3	5	2	8	4
5	6	3	1	7	9	4	2	8
9	8	4	3	6	2	5	1	7
2	1	7	8	5	4	6	3	9
8	4	5	6	2	3	9	7	1
3	7	6	5	9	1	8	4	2
1	2	9	4	8	7	3	5	6

235

1	6	2	8	3	7	5	4	9
3	7	5	1	9	4	2	8	6
4	9	8	6	5	2	1	7	3
6	8	9	3	2	1	4	5	7
7	5	3	4	6	8	9	2	1
2	4	1	5	7	9	3	6	8
5	1	6	2	8	3	7	9	4
9	2	4	7	1	6	8	3	5
8	3	7	9	4	5	6	1	2

236

4	5	3	7	2	9	8	1	6
2	1	6	3	5	8	9	7	4
8	9	7	1	6	4	2	3	5
3	2	1	5	9	6	4	8	7
7	6	8	4	3	1	5	9	2
5	4	9	8	7	2	1	6	3
1	3	2	6	8	5	7	4	9
6	8	5	9	4	7	3	2	1
9	7	4	2	1	3	6	5	8

237

6	7	1	4	5	2	9	3	8
8	2	4	7	9	3	6	5	1
9	5	3	6	8	1	7	2	4
5	9	8	1	4	6	2	7	3
7	4	2	9	3	5	1	8	6
1	3	6	2	7	8	4	9	5
4	8	9	5	6	7	3	1	2
2	6	5	3	1	9	8	4	7
3	1	7	8	2	4	5	6	9

238

5	3	4	7	1	6	2	8	9
7	8	9	3	5	2	1	4	6
2	6	1	9	8	4	7	5	3
3	9	6	5	7	8	4	2	1
1	5	2	4	3	9	8	6	7
4	7	8	6	2	1	9	3	5
9	2	7	8	6	5	3	1	4
8	4	5	1	9	3	6	7	2
6	1	3	2	4	7	5	9	8

239

2	3	5	4	7	8	1	6	9
6	7	8	1	5	9	4	2	3
1	9	4	2	6	3	8	5	7
7	2	3	8	9	5	6	4	1
9	8	1	7	4	6	5	3	2
5	4	6	3	1	2	7	9	8
4	1	2	5	3	7	9	8	6
3	6	7	9	8	4	2	1	5
8	5	9	6	2	1	3	7	4

240

1	8	6	2	3	5	4	7	9
7	4	5	8	1	9	3	6	2
9	3	2	7	4	6	5	1	8
8	7	4	5	9	1	6	2	3
3	2	9	6	8	7	1	5	4
6	5	1	4	2	3	8	9	7
5	6	3	9	7	8	2	4	1
4	9	8	1	6	2	7	3	5
2	1	7	3	5	4	9	8	6

241

4	1	8	2	3	7	9	5	6
7	3	9	8	5	6	4	1	2
2	5	6	1	4	9	7	3	8
6	7	4	3	1	2	8	9	5
5	2	1	6	9	8	3	7	4
8	9	3	4	7	5	2	6	1
9	4	2	5	6	3	1	8	7
1	6	7	9	8	4	5	2	3
3	8	5	7	2	1	6	4	9

242

6	7	1	9	4	5	8	2	3
9	5	2	8	1	3	6	7	4
4	3	8	2	7	6	9	5	1
8	4	7	3	9	2	5	1	6
2	1	9	5	6	7	4	3	8
5	6	3	4	8	1	7	9	2
3	9	4	1	5	8	2	6	7
1	8	6	7	2	9	3	4	5
7	2	5	6	3	4	1	8	9

243

2	1	8	4	5	3	7	6	9
6	5	9	1	7	2	4	3	8
3	7	4	8	9	6	2	5	1
1	2	6	3	8	9	5	7	4
8	9	3	7	4	5	6	1	2
5	4	7	2	6	1	9	8	3
4	6	5	9	1	8	3	2	7
7	3	1	5	2	4	8	9	6
9	8	2	6	3	7	1	4	5

244

2	8	5	6	7	1	9	3	4
9	1	3	5	4	2	8	6	7
4	6	7	3	9	8	5	1	2
8	5	6	2	3	4	7	9	1
1	3	4	9	5	7	2	8	6
7	9	2	8	1	6	3	4	5
3	4	9	7	6	5	1	2	8
6	7	8	1	2	9	4	5	3
5	2	1	4	8	3	6	7	9

245

5	6	4	1	7	2	8	3	9
1	9	3	4	6	8	7	5	2
2	7	8	5	9	3	1	4	6
7	2	1	8	4	5	6	9	3
4	3	6	2	1	9	5	8	7
9	8	5	7	3	6	4	2	1
8	5	7	9	2	1	3	6	4
6	4	2	3	5	7	9	1	8
3	1	9	6	8	4	2	7	5

246

3	6	4	1	8	5	2	9	7
1	8	2	3	9	7	6	4	5
9	7	5	2	4	6	1	3	8
8	5	3	4	1	9	7	6	2
6	4	7	8	5	2	9	1	3
2	9	1	7	6	3	8	5	4
7	1	9	5	3	8	4	2	6
5	2	6	9	7	4	3	8	1
4	3	8	6	2	1	5	7	9